EASY PIANO

HIT SONGS
IN EASY KEYS

"Hit Songs in Easy Keys" include no more than one sharp or one flat in the **key**
The key signature appears on the left side of every staff, right next to the clef signs.

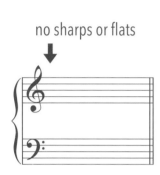

no sharps or flats

one sharp: F♯
all Fs are played as F♯

one flat: B♭
all Bs are played as B♭

Sometimes **accidenta**s and flats not in the key signature.
An accidental alte   measure. The next bar line or a
                                      ccidental.

F♯ (in key signature)   F♮

ISBN 978-1-70514-256-1

Hal•Leonard®
7777 W. BLUEMOUND RD. P.O. BOX 13819 MILWAUKEE, WI 53213

Visit Hal Leonard Online at
www.halleonard.com

Contact us:
Hal Leonard
7777 West Bluemound Road
Milwaukee, WI 53213
Email: info@halleonard.com

In Europe, contact:
Hal Leonard Europe Limited
42 Wigmore Street
Marylebone, London, W1U 2RN
Email: info@halleonardeurope.com

In Australia, contact:
Hal Leonard Australia Pty. Ltd.
4 Lentara Court
Cheltenham, Victoria, 3192 Australia
Email: info@halleonard.com.au

ADORE YOU

Words and Music by HARRY STYLES,
THOMAS HULL, TYLER JOHNSON
and AMY ALLEN

Moderate Pop Rock

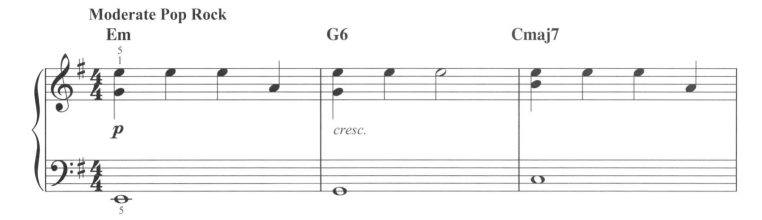

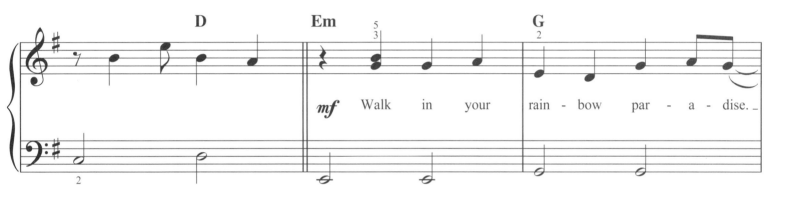

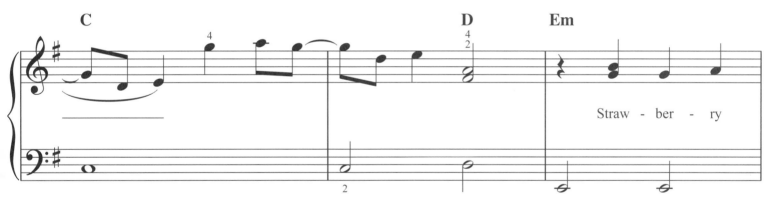

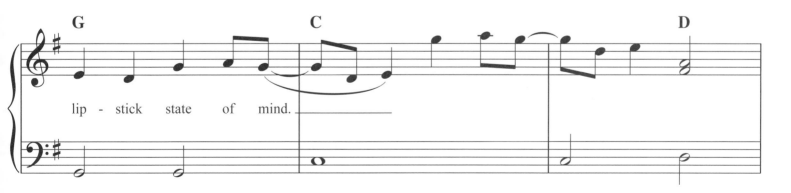

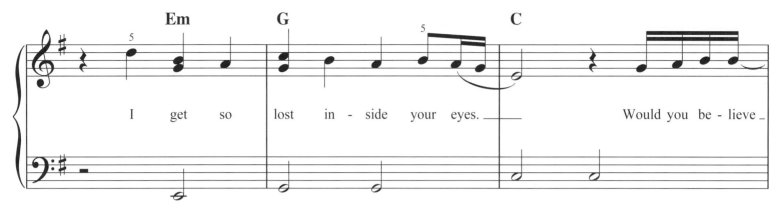

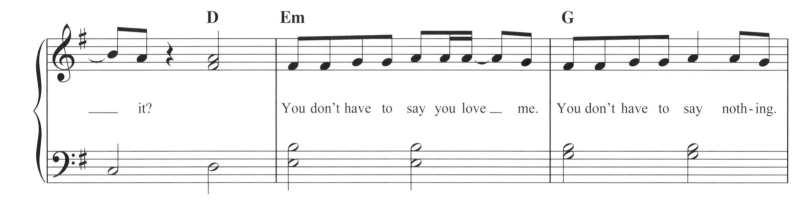

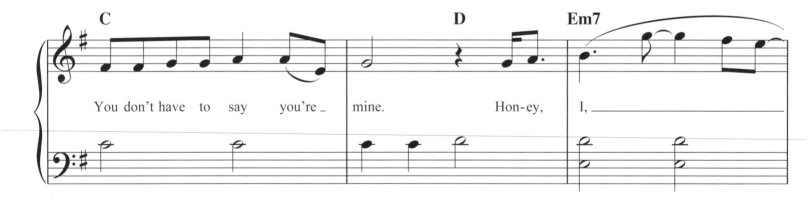

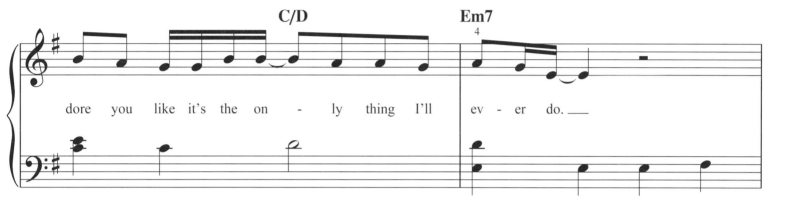

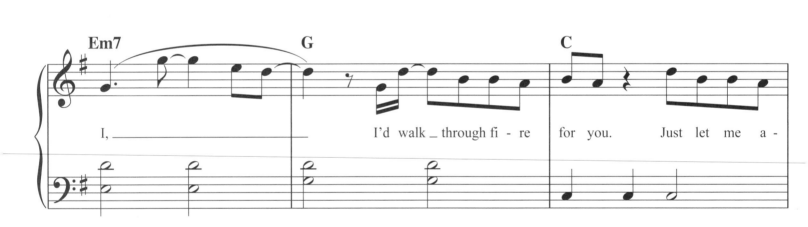

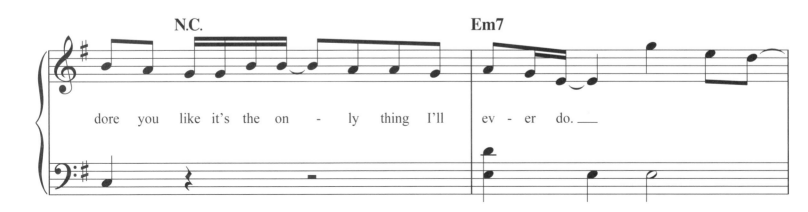

I'd walk _ through fi - re for you. Just let me a - dore you. Oh, hon-ey,

I, _ I'd walk _ through fi - re for you. Just let me a -

dore you. Oh, hon-ey.

Just let me a - dore you like it's the on - ly thing I'll ev - er do. _

AFTERGLOW

Words and Music by ED SHEERAN,
DAVID HODGES and FRED GIBSON

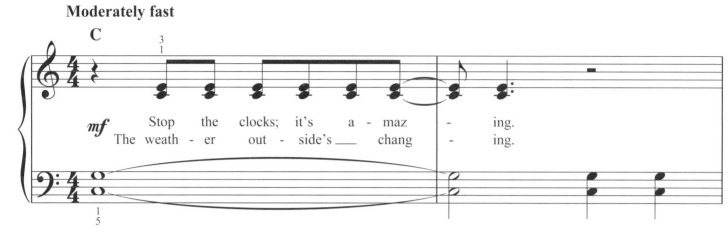

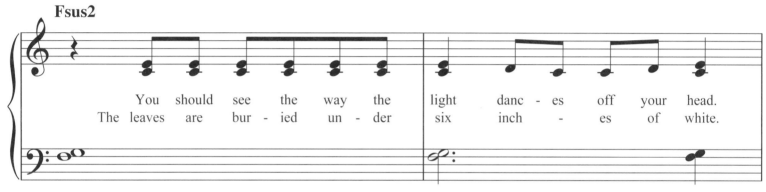

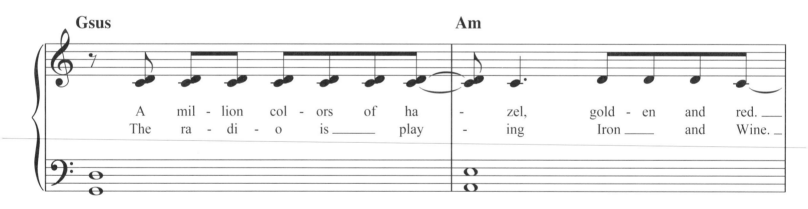

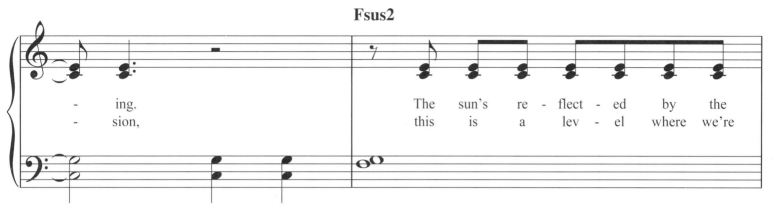

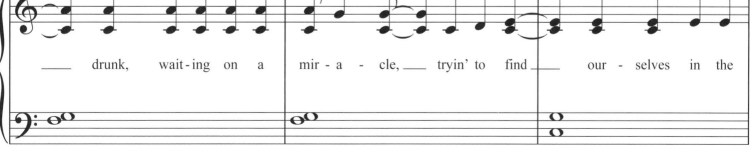

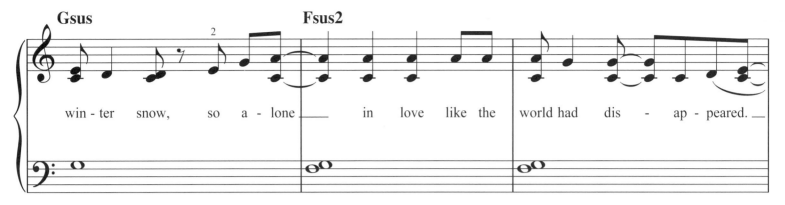

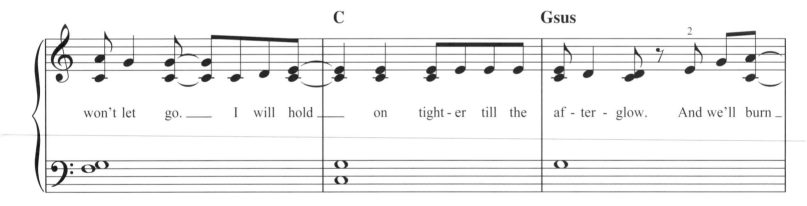

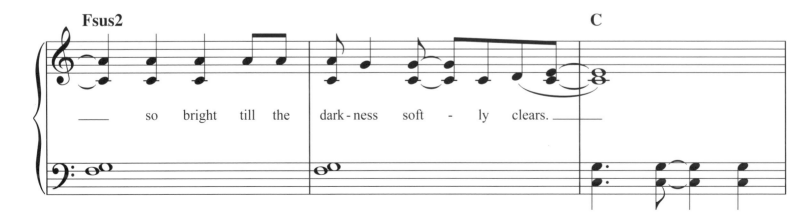

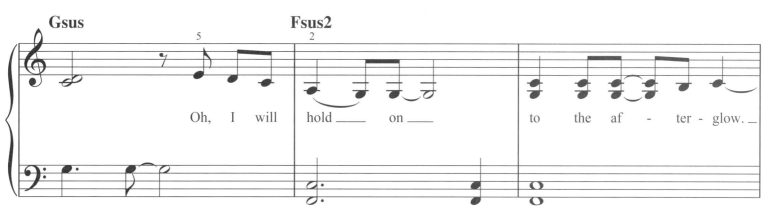

Oh, I will hold ____ on ____ to the af - ter - glow. ___

Oh, I will hold ____ on ____

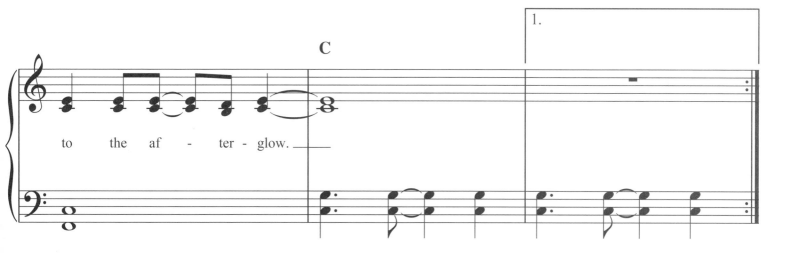

to the af - ter - glow. ___

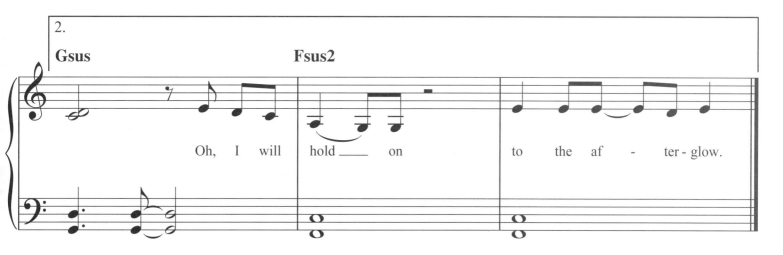

Oh, I will hold ____ on to the af - ter - glow.

ANYONE

Words and Music by JUSTIN BIEBER,
JON BELLION, JORDAN JOHNSON,
ALEXANDER IZQUIERDO, ANDREW WATT,
RAUL CUBINA, STEFAN JOHNSON
and MICHAEL POLLACK

Moderate Pop

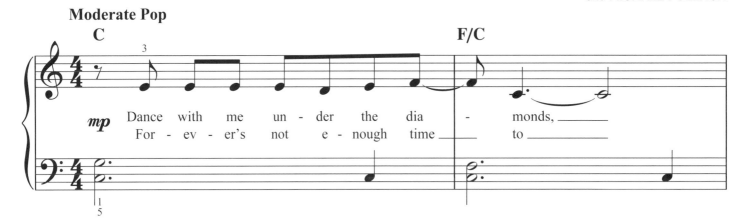

Dance with me un-der the dia - monds,
For - ev - er's not e - nough time to

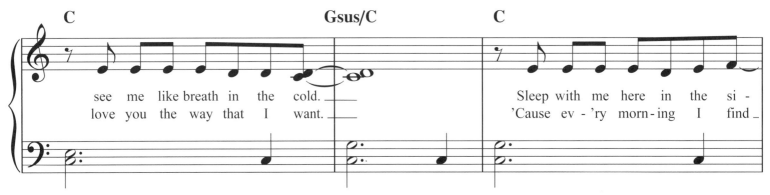

see me like breath in the cold.
love you the way that I want.

Sleep with me here in the si -
'Cause ev - 'ry morn-ing I find

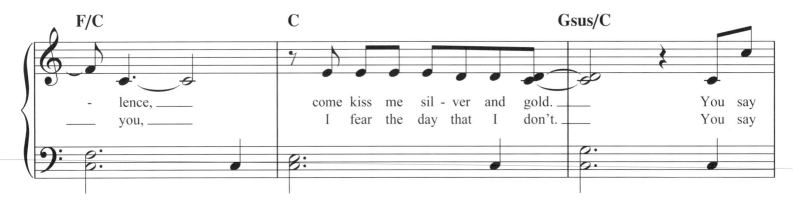

- lence,
you,

come kiss me sil - ver and gold.
I fear the day that I don't.

You say
You say

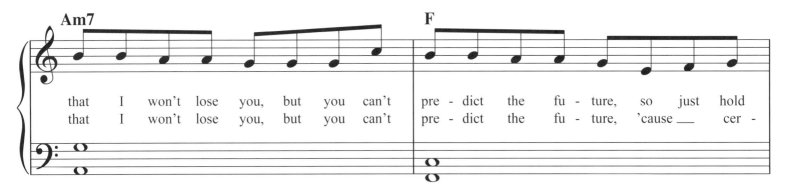

that I won't lose you, but you can't
that I won't lose you, but you can't

pre - dict the fu - ture, so just hold
pre - dict the fu - ture, 'cause cer -

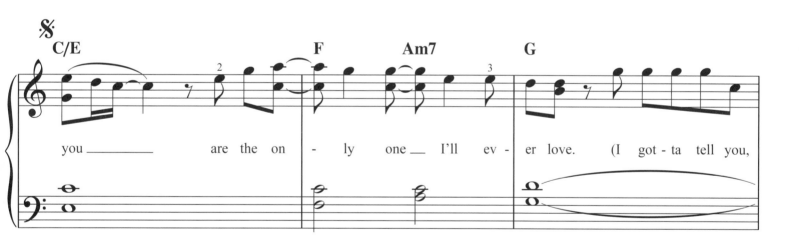

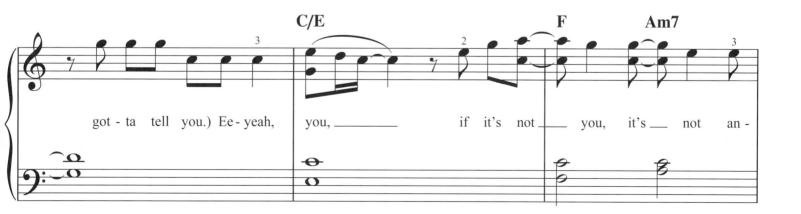

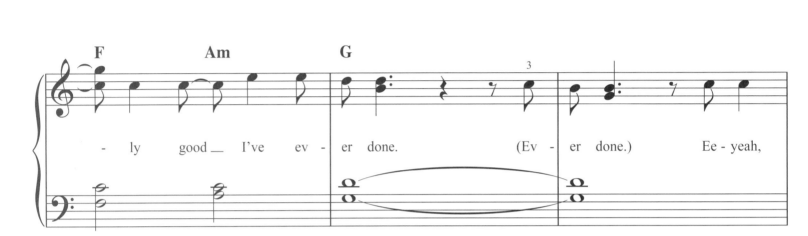

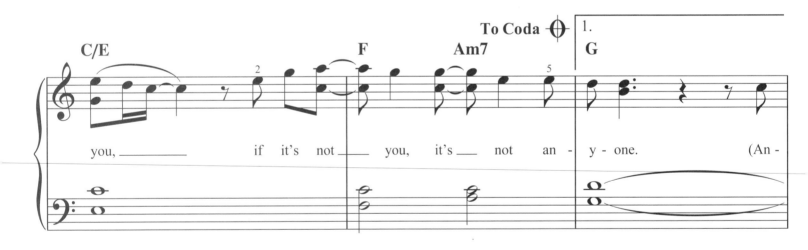

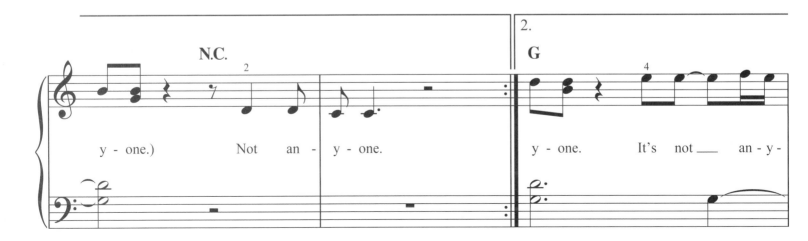

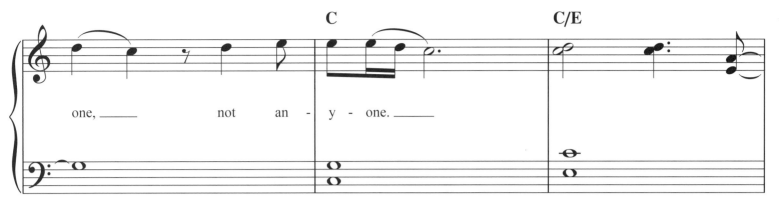

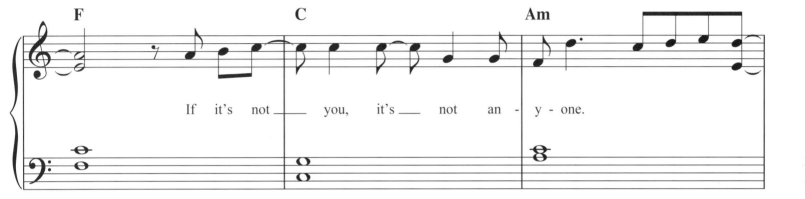

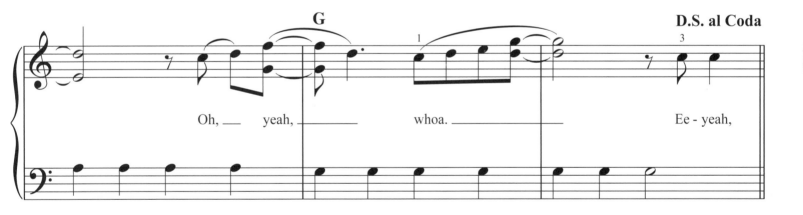

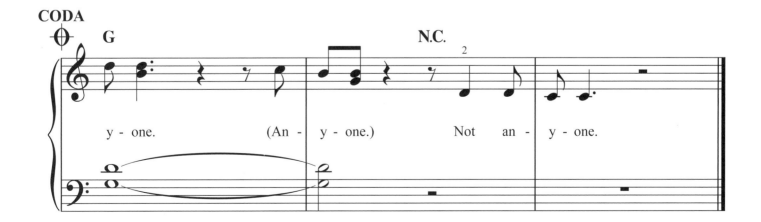

BETTER DAYS

Words and Music by RYAN TEDDER,
BRENT KUTZLE and JOHN NATHANIEL

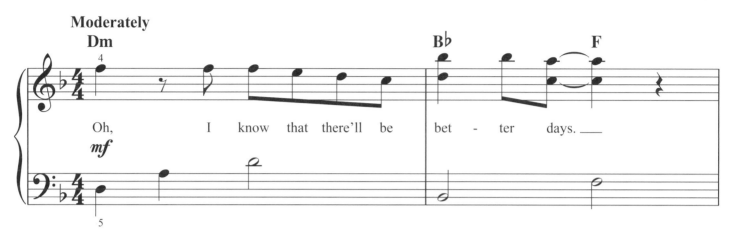

Oh, I know that there'll be bet - ter days. ___

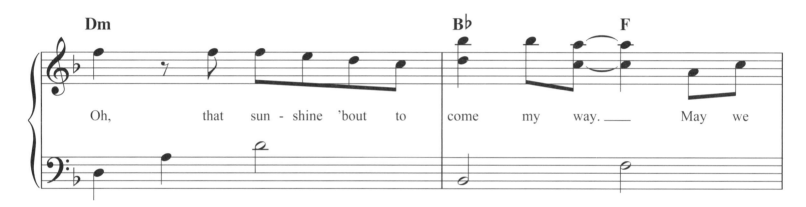

Oh, that sun - shine 'bout to come my way. ___ May we

nev - er, ev - er shed an - oth - er tear for to - day, ___ 'cause,

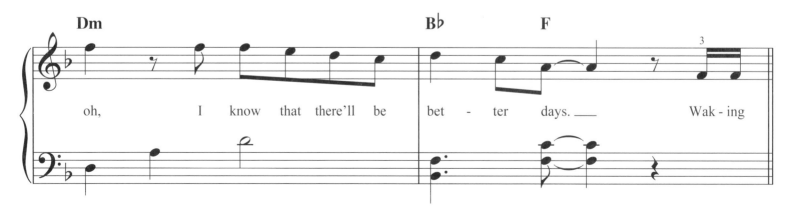

oh, I know that there'll be bet - ter days. ___ Wak - ing

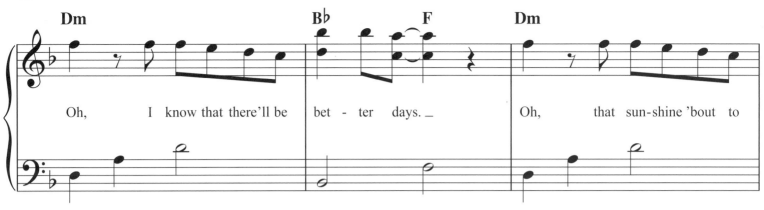

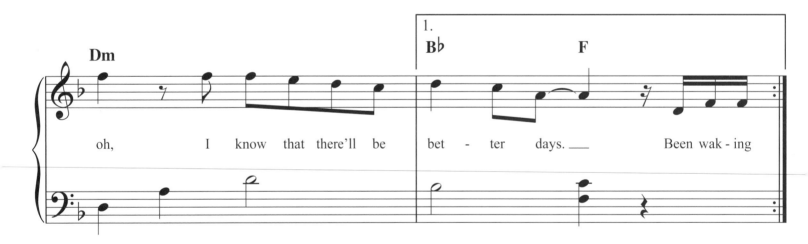

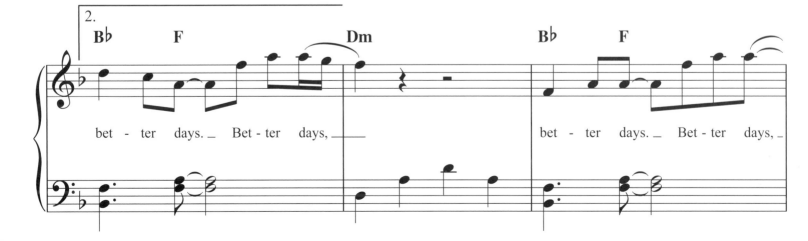

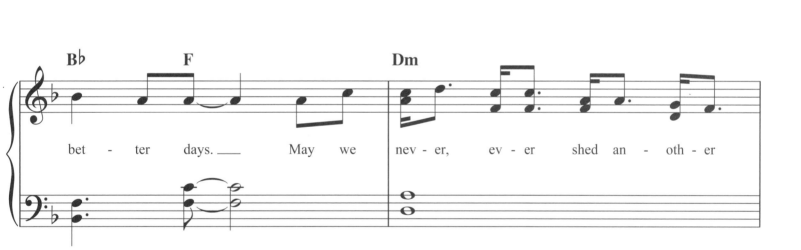

BLINDING LIGHTS

Words and Music by ABEL TESFAYE,
MAX MARTIN, JASON QUENNEVILLE,
OSCAR HOLTER and AHMAD BALSHE

Fast dance beat

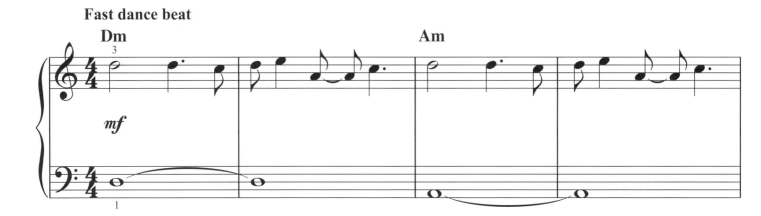

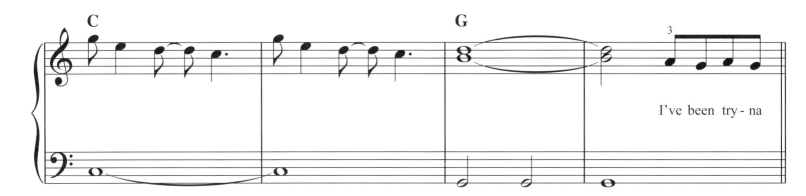

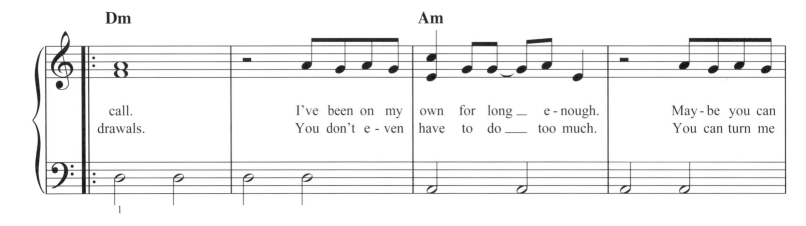

show me how __ to love,
on with just __ a touch,
may -
ba -
be. _____
by. _____
I'm go - in' through with -
(I look a - round, but)

Sin Cit - y's cold __ and emp - ty.
(Ah.) No one's a - round __ to judge me.

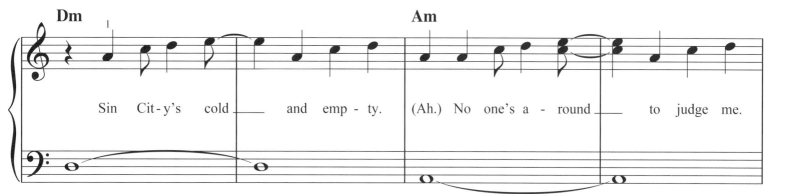

(Ah.) I can't see clear - ly when you're __ go - o - one. I said,

ooh, _____ I'm __ blind - ed by __ the lights. _____ No,

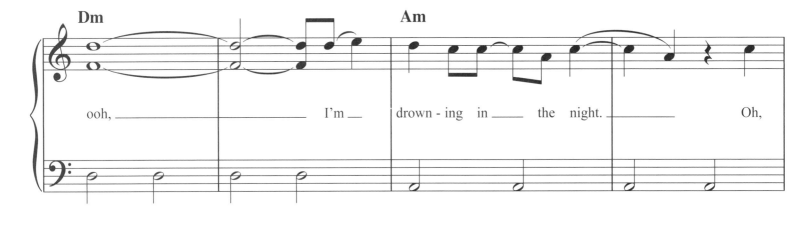

(Hey, hey, hey.)

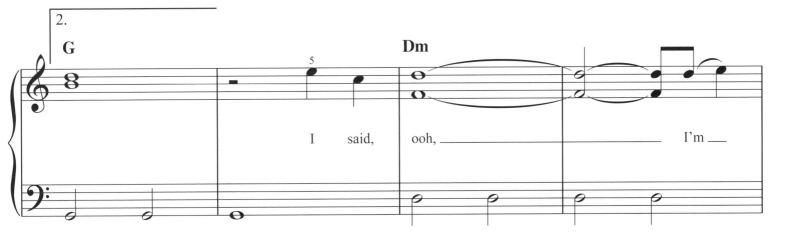

I said, ooh, _____ I'm _____

blind - ed by ___ the lights. ___ No, I can't sleep ___ un -

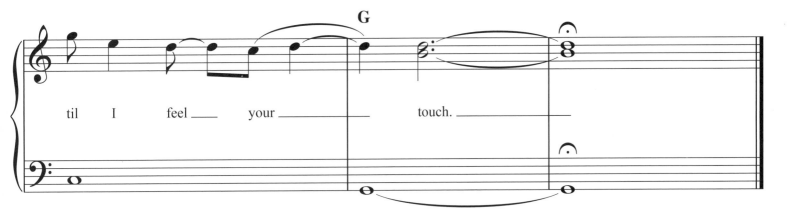

til I feel ___ your _____ touch. _____

DESPACITO

Words and Music by LUIS FONSI,
ERIKA ENDER, JUSTIN BIEBER,
JASON BOYD, MARTY JAMES GARTON
and RAMÓN AYALA

Come on o - ver in my di - rec - tion.

So thank-ful for that, it's such a bless - in', yeah. Turn ev-'ry sit - u -

a - tion in - to heav - en, yeah. Oh, oh, you

are my sun - rise on the dark - est day. Got me feel-in' some kind of

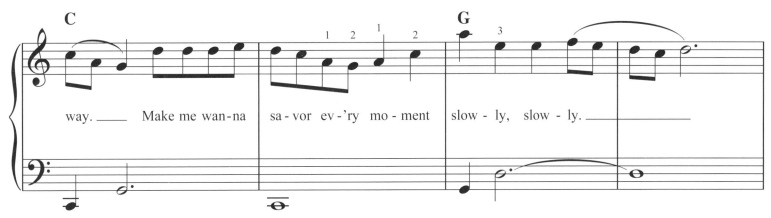

way. ___ Make me wan-na sa-vor ev -'ry mo - ment slow - ly, slow - ly. ___

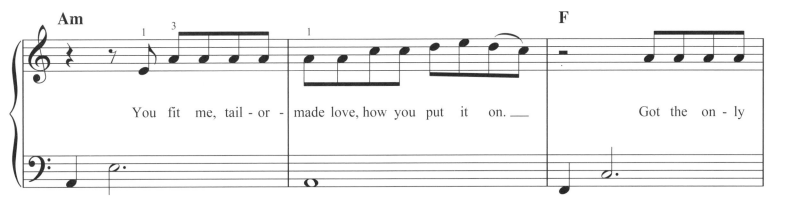

You fit me, tail-or - made love, how you put it on. ___ Got the on - ly

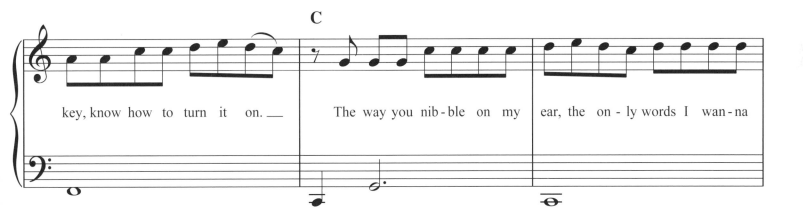

key, know how to turn it on. ___ The way you nib-ble on my ear, the on - ly words I wan-na

hear: Ba - by, take it slow so we can last long. ___ Tú tú e - res el i -

mán y yo soy el me - tal. Me voy a - cer - can-do y voy ar - man-do el

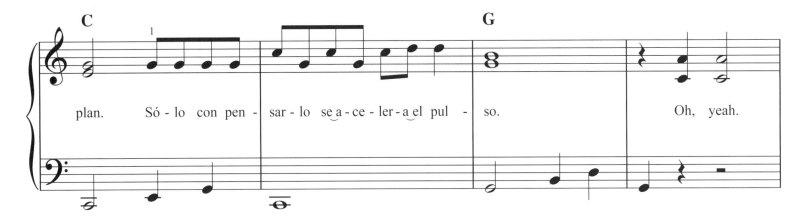

plan. Só - lo con pen - sar - lo se a - ce - ler-a el pul - so. Oh, yeah.

Ya, ya me es - tá gus - tan - do más de lo nor - mal. To - dos mis sen

ti - dos van pi - dien - do más. Es-to hay que to - mar - lo sin nin - gún a - pu -

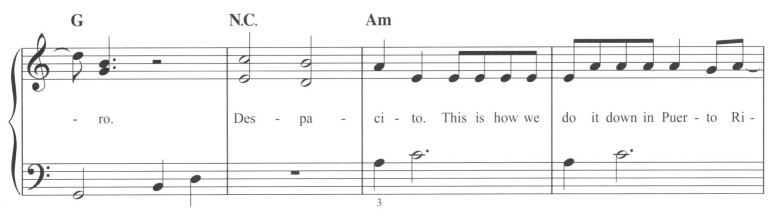

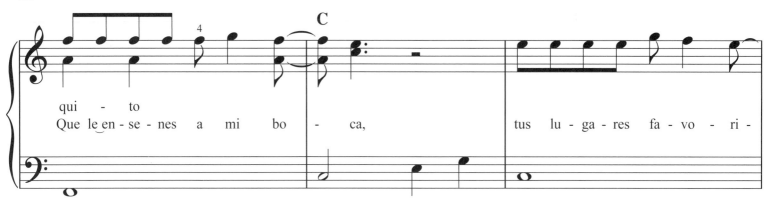

qui - to
Que le en - se - nes a mi bo - ca, tus lu - ga - res fa - vo - ri -

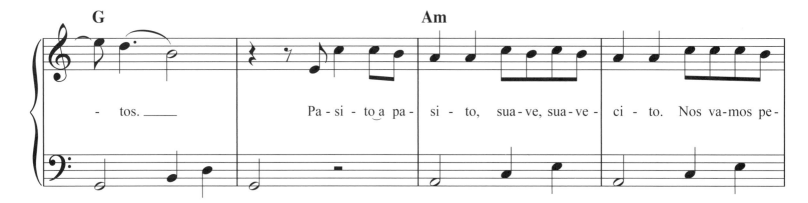

- tos. _____ Pa - si - to a pa - si - to, sua - ve, sua - ve - ci - to. Nos va - mos pe -

gan - do po - qui - to a po - qui - to
Has - ta pro - vo - car tus gri - tos.

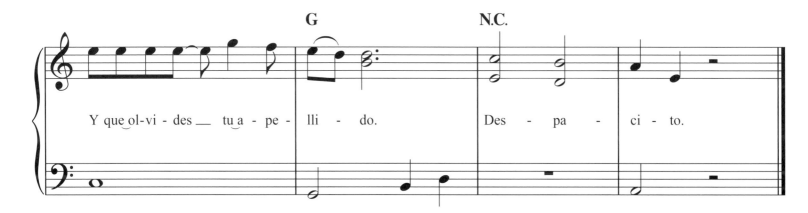

Y que ol - vi - des __ tu a - pe - lli - do. Des - pa - ci - to.

DRIVERS LICENSE

Words and Music by OLIVIA RODRIGO
and DANIEL NIGRO

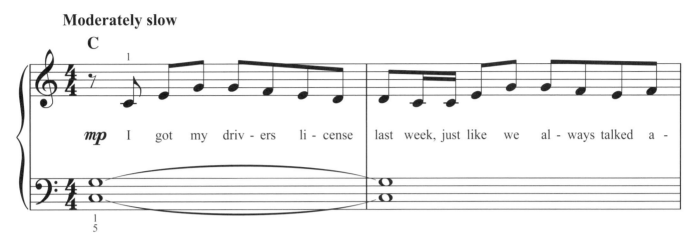

day I drove through the sub - urbs, 'cause how could I ev - er love some - one

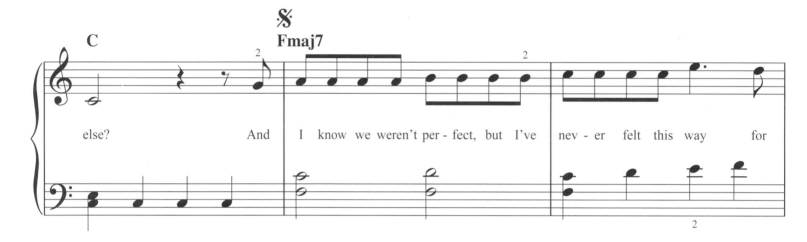

else? And I know we weren't per - fect, but I've nev - er felt this way for

no one. And I just can't i - mag - ine how you could be so o - kay ___ now that

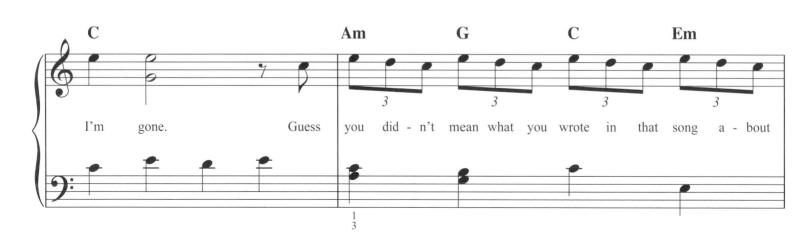

I'm gone. Guess you did - n't mean what you wrote in that song a - bout

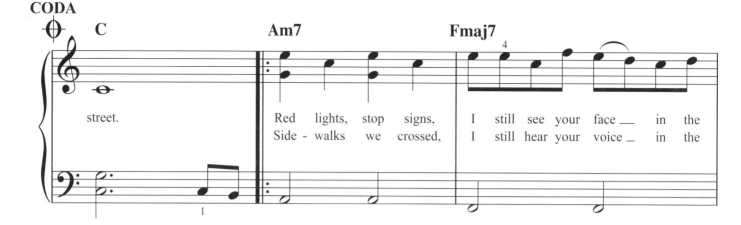

CODA

street.

Red lights, stop signs,
Side - walks we crossed,

I still see your face ___ in the
I still hear your voice ___ in the

white cars, front yards.
traf - fic; we're laugh - ing

Can't drive past the plac - es we
o - ver all the noise. ___ God, I'm

used to go to, 'cause
so blue, know we're through, but

I still ___ love you, babe. ___
I still ___ love you, babe. ___

I know we weren't per - fect, but I've

nev - er felt this way for

no one. And

GIRLS LIKE YOU

Words and Music by ADAM LEVINE,
BRITTANY HAZZARD, JASON EVIGAN
GIAN STONE and HENRY WALTER

Moderately fast half-time beat

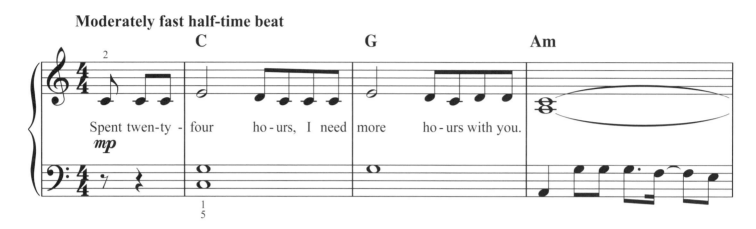

Spent twen-ty - four ho - urs, I need more ho - urs with you.

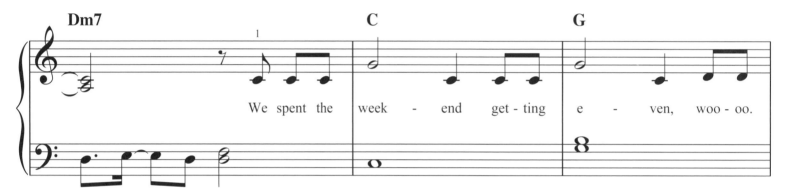

We spent the week - end get - ting e - ven, woo - oo.

We spent the late _____ nights mak-ing

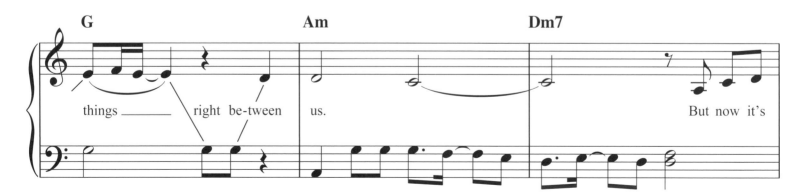

things _____ right be-tween us. But now it's

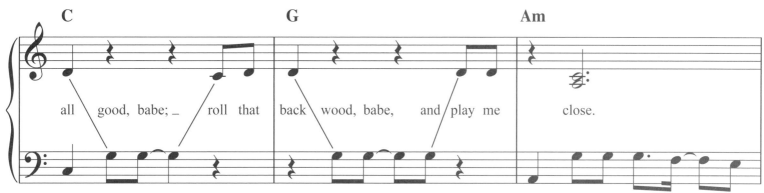

all good, babe; _ roll that back wood, babe, and play me close.

'Cause girls like you run 'round with guys like me till sun-down. When

I come through, I need a girl like you, yeah, yeah. Girls like you love fun, and

yeah, me too, what I ____ want. When I come through, I need a girl like you, yeah, yeah.

Yeah, yeah, yeah,　　yeah, yeah, yeah,　　I need a

girl like you, yeah, yeah.　　Yeah, yeah, yeah,　　yeah, yeah,

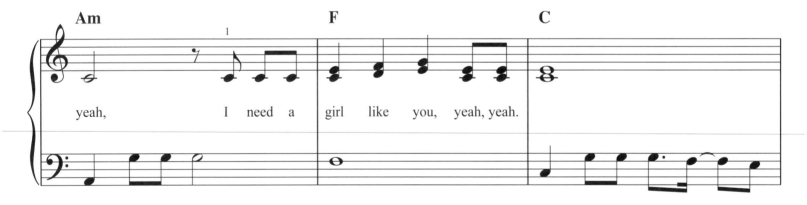

yeah,　　I need a　girl like you, yeah, yeah.

I HOPE

Words and Music by GABBY BARRETT,
ZACHARY KALE and JON NITE

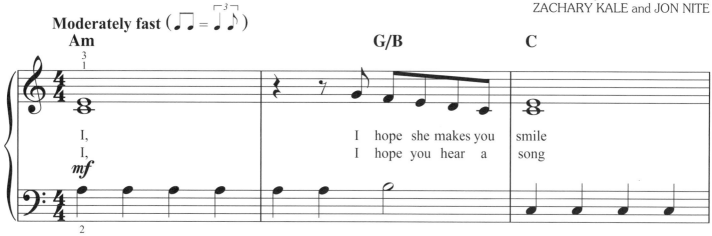

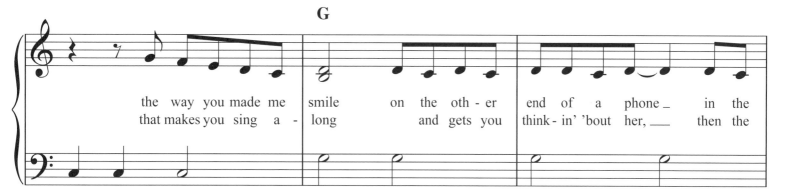

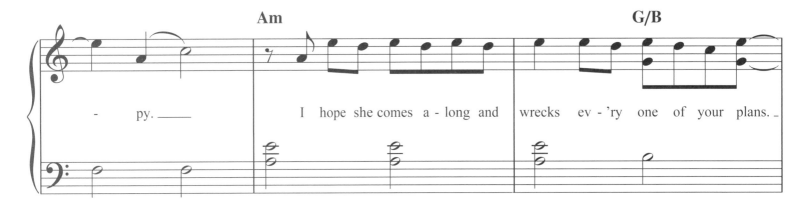

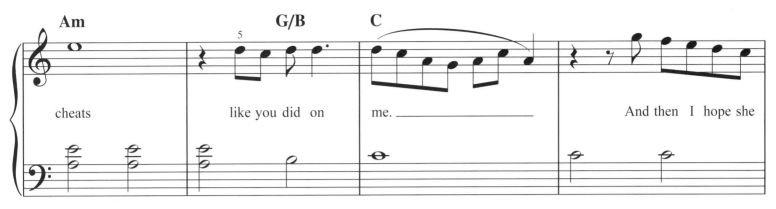

cheats | like you did on | me. _____ | And then I hope she

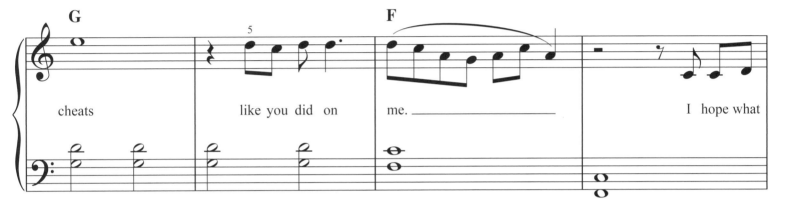

cheats | like you did on | me. _____ | I hope what

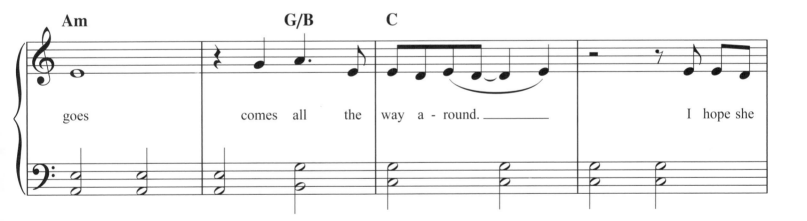

goes | comes all the way a - round. _____ | I hope she

makes you feel the same way a - bout her that I feel a - bout you right now. _____

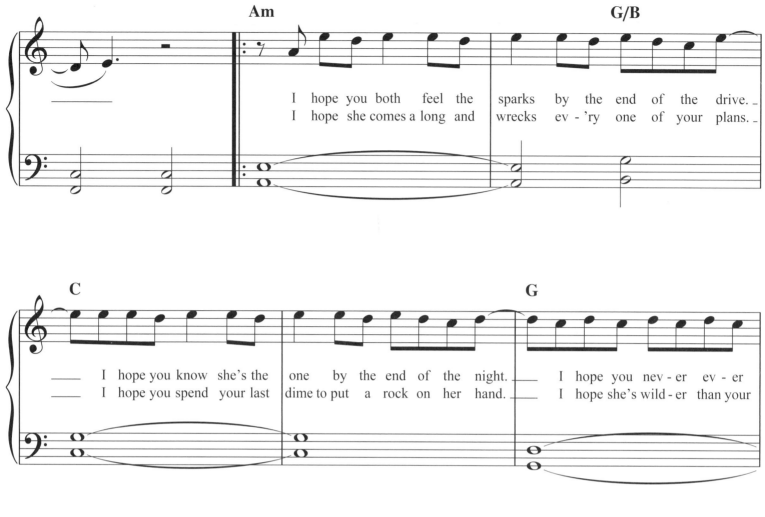

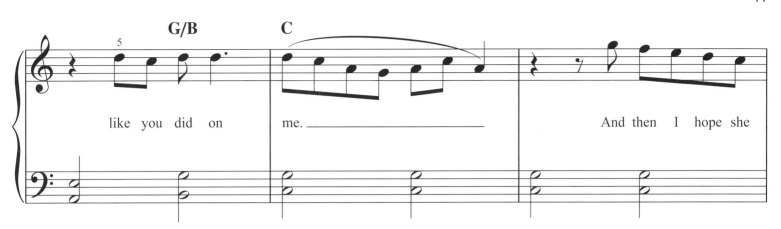

like you did on me. _____ And then I hope she

cheats like you did on me, _____

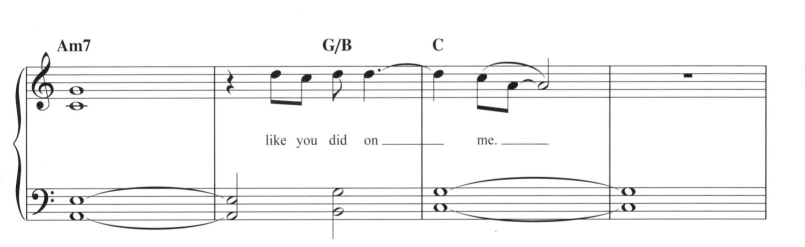

like you did on _____ me. _____

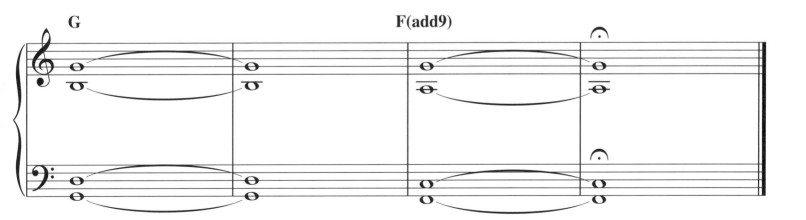

HOLD ON TO ME

Words and Music by LAUREN DAIGLE,
PAUL DUNCAN and PAUL MABURY

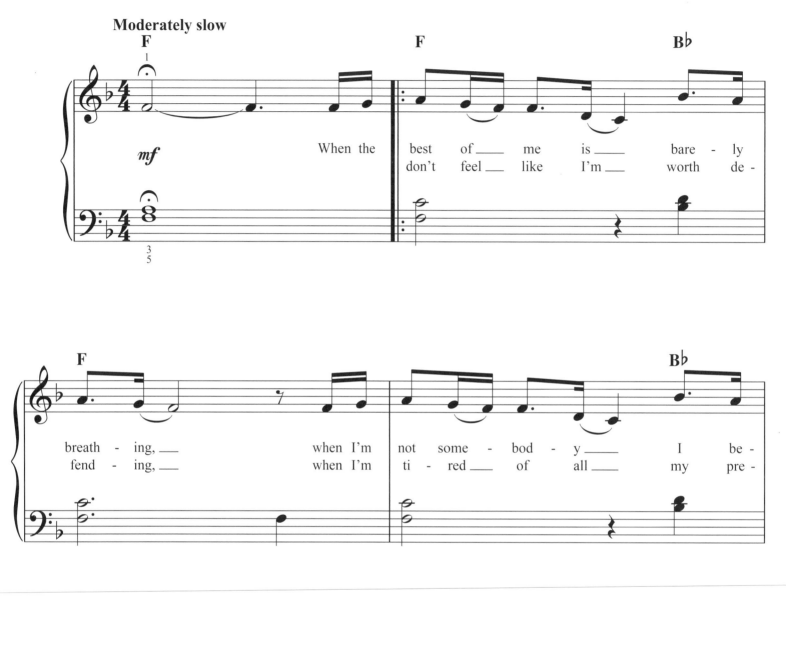

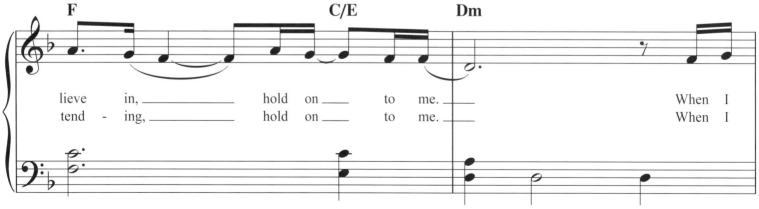

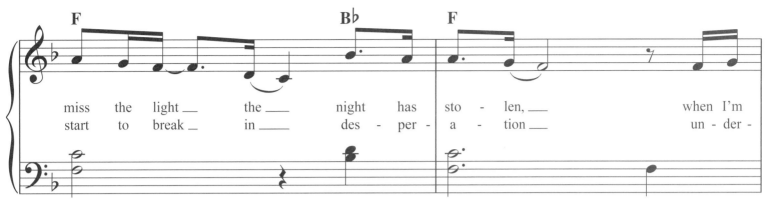

miss the light ___ the ___ night has sto - len, ___   when I'm
start to break ___ in ___ des - per - a - tion ___   un - der -

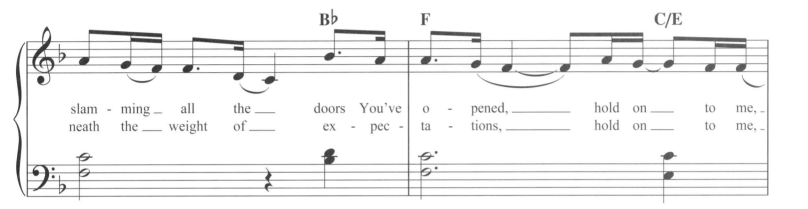

slam - ming ___ all the ___ doors You've o - pened, _____ hold on ___ to me, ___
neath the ___ weight of ___ ex - pec - ta - tions, _____ hold on ___ to me, ___

hold on ___ to me.
hold on ___ to me.

Hold on to me ___ when it's too dark to see ___

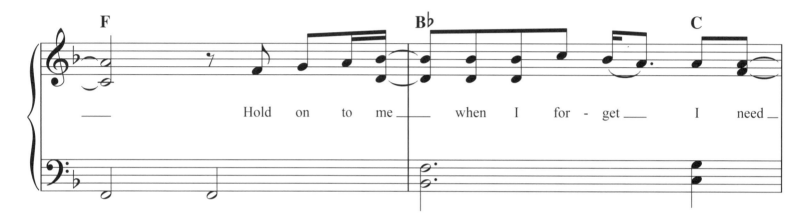

I could rest here ___ in Your ___ arms for-

ev - er _____ 'cause I know no - bod - y ___ loves me

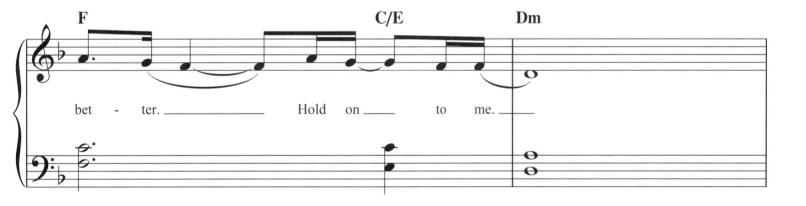

bet - ter. _____ Hold on ___ to me. ___

Hold on ___ to me. ___

HOLY

Words and Music by JUSTIN BIEBER,
JON BELLION, ANTHONY JONES,
TOMMY BROWN, STEVEN FRANKS,
MICHAEL POLLACK, JORGEN ODEGARD
and CHANCELOR BENNETT

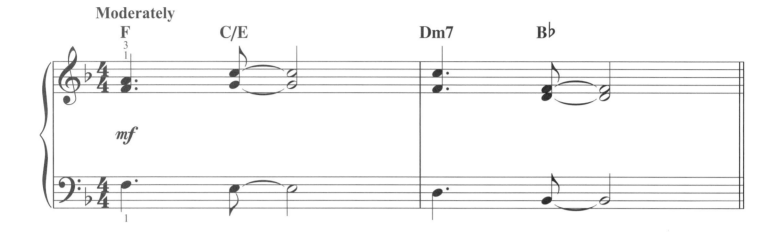

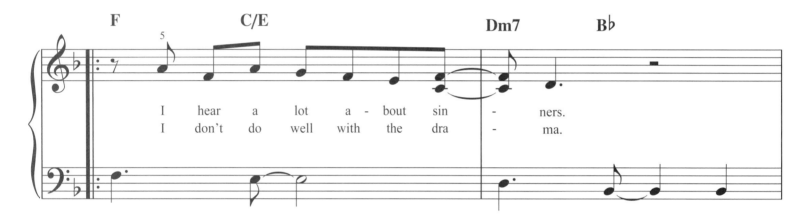

I hear a lot a-bout sin - ners.
I don't do well with the dra - ma.

Don't think that I'll be a saint.
No, I can't stand it be-ing fake.

No, no, no, no, no, no, no,

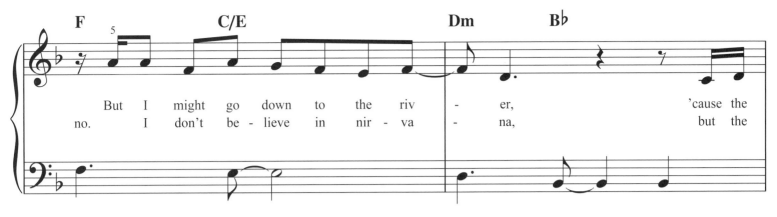

But I might go down to the riv - er, 'cause the
no. I don't be - lieve in nir - va - na,

way that the sky o - pens up when we touch, yeah, it's mak - ing me say that the way you
way that we love in the night gave me life, ba - by. I can't ex - plain

hold me, hold me, hold me, hold me, hold me feels so

ho - ly, ho - ly, ho - ly, ho - ly, ho - ly. Oh God,

run - ning to the al - tar like a track star. Can't wait an - oth - er sec - ond 'cause the way you

1.

hold me, hold __ me, hold me, hold me, hold me feels so _____ ho - ly.

2.

hold me, hold __ me, hold me, hold me, hold me feels so

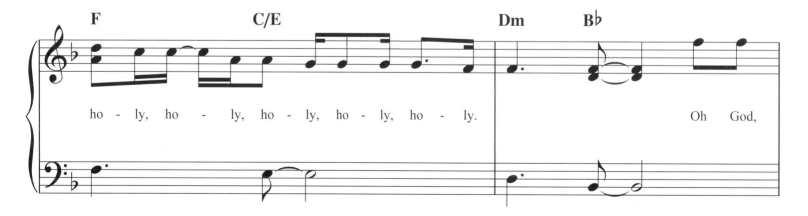

ho - ly, ho - ly, ho - ly, ho - ly, ho - ly. Oh God,

running to the altar like a track star. Can't wait an-oth-er sec-ond, oh God.

Run-ning to the al-tar like a track star. Can't wait an-oth-er sec-ond, oh God.

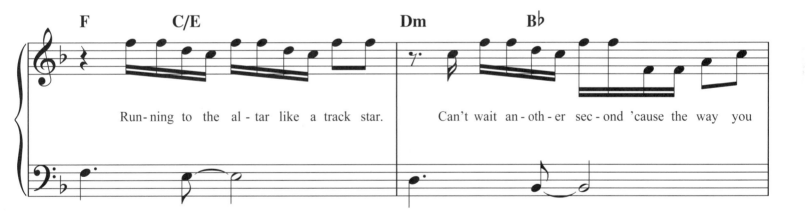

Run-ning to the al-tar like a track star. Can't wait an-oth-er sec-ond 'cause the way you

hold me, hold __ me, hold me, hold me feels so ho - ly.

OLD TOWN ROAD
(Remix)

Words and Music by TRENT REZNOR,
BILLY RAY CYRUS, JOCELYN DONALD,
ATTICUS ROSS, KIOWA ROUKEMA
and MONTERO LAMAR HILL

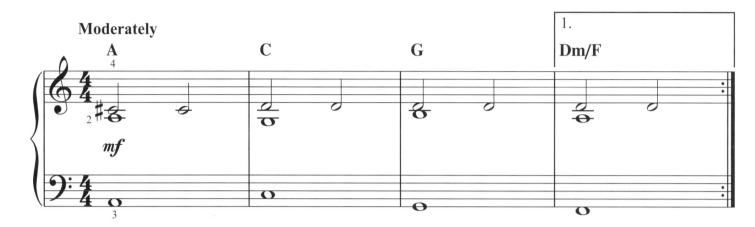

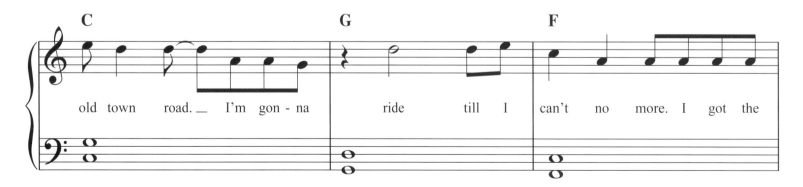

hors - es in the back, horse tack is at-tached. Hat is mat - te black, got the

boots that's black to match. _____ Rid - in' on a horse, you can whip your Porsche.

I been in the val - ley, you ain't been up off the porch, __ now.

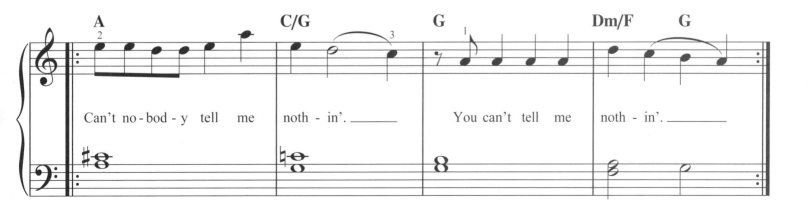

Can't no - bod - y tell me noth - in'. _____ You can't tell me noth - in'. _____

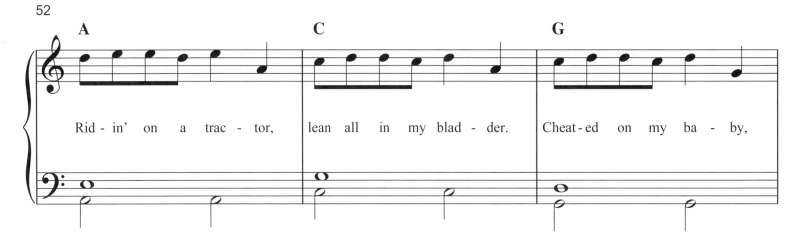

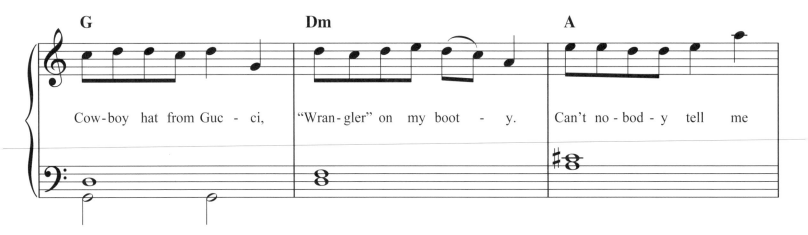

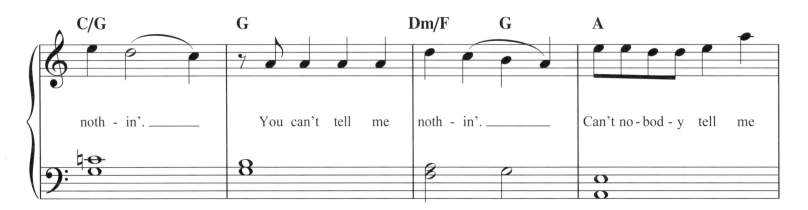

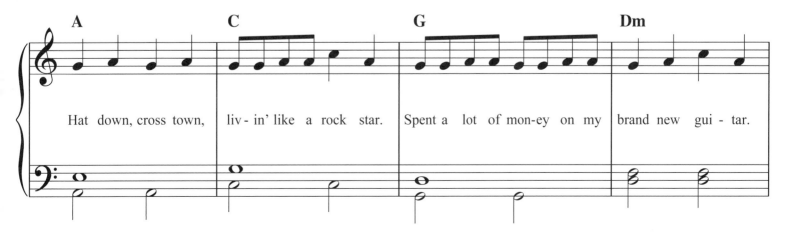

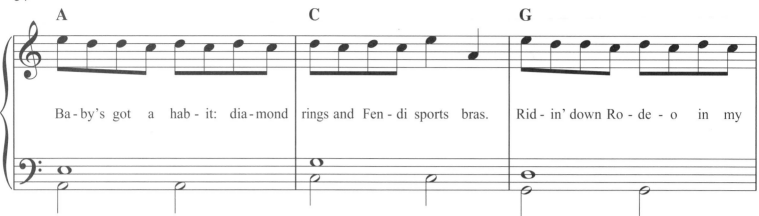

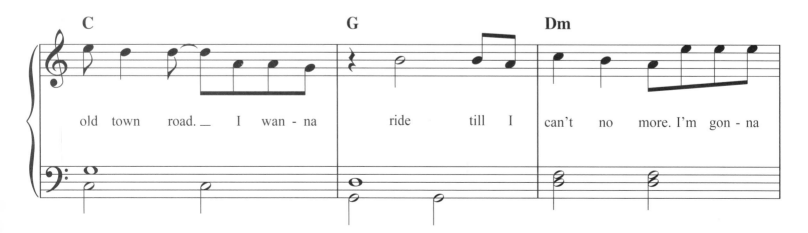

take my horse to the old town road. __ I'm gon-na ride till I can't no more. I'm gon-na

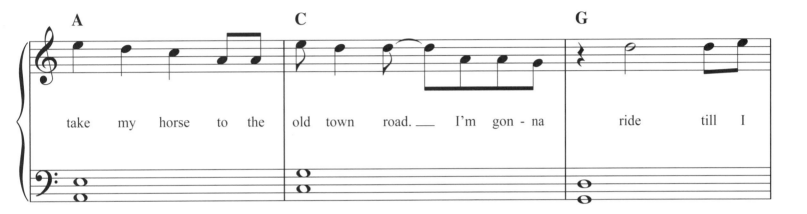

take my horse to the old town road. __ I'm gon-na ride till I

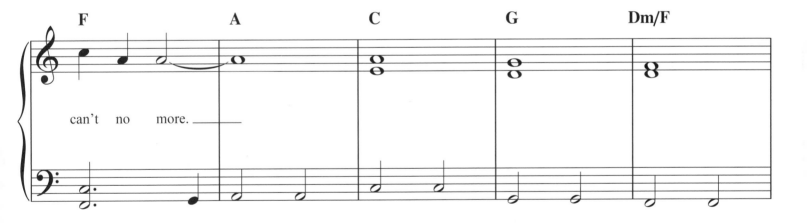

can't no more. __

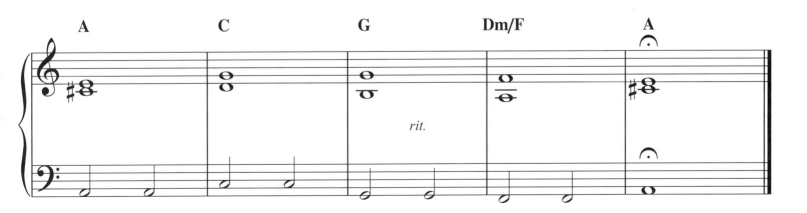

rit.

PERFECT

Words and Music by
ED SHEERAN

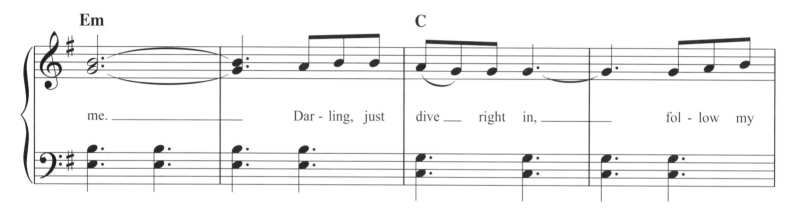

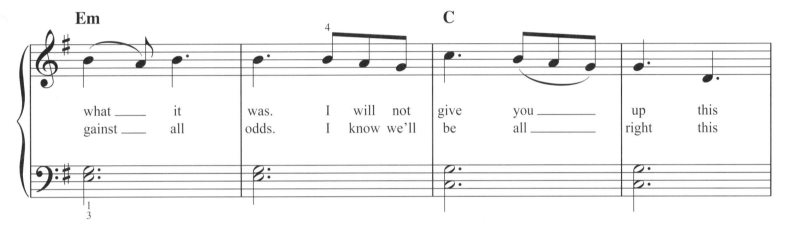

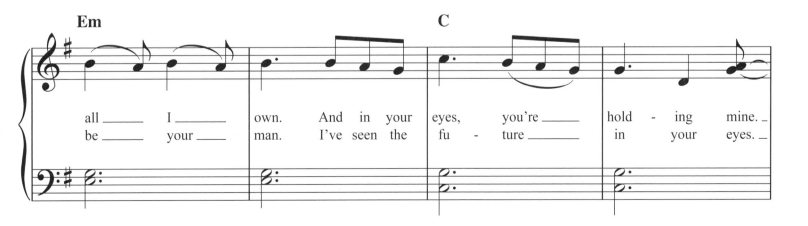

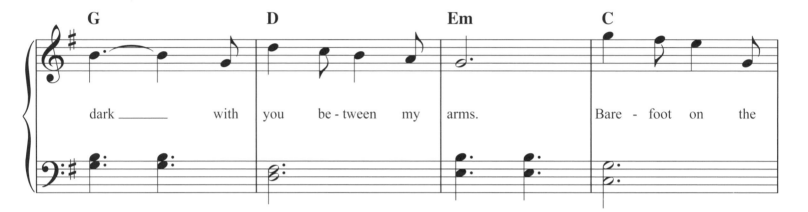

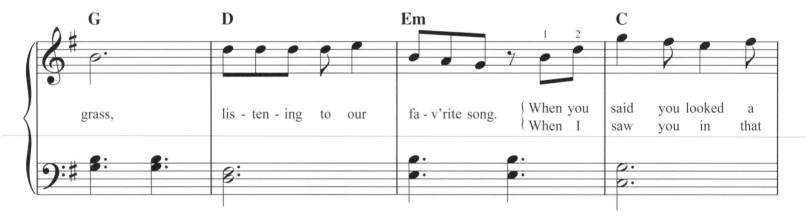

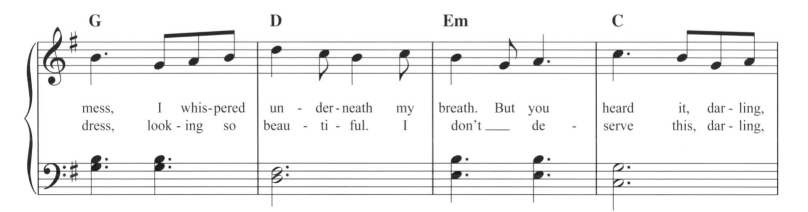

you   look   per - fect   to - night.____
you   look   per - fect   to - night.____

To Coda

Well, I   found a   wom - an, _____   strong - er than

an - y - one I   know.____   She shares my   dreams, I   hope __ that   some - day   I'll share her

home. _____   I found a   love _____   to car - ry

more than just my se - crets, to car - ry love, to car - y chil - dren ____ of our

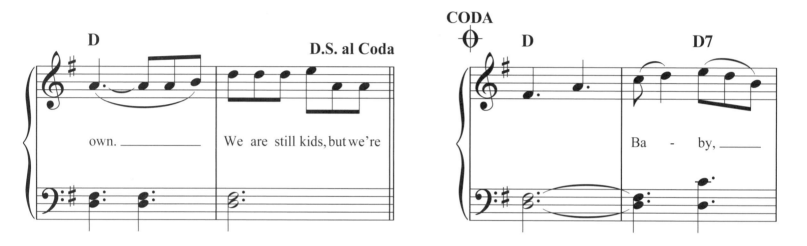

own. ____ We are still kids, but we're

CODA

Ba - by, ____

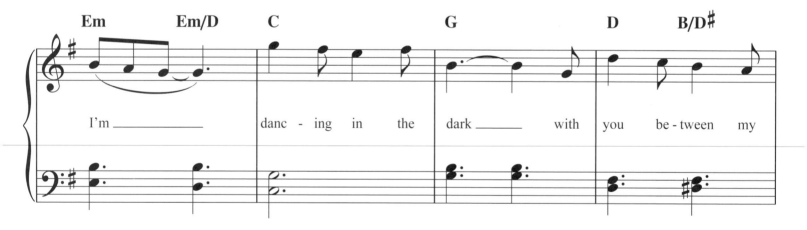

I'm ____ danc - ing in the dark ____ with you be - tween my

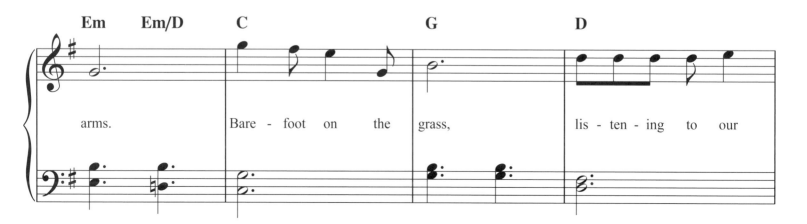

arms. Bare - foot on the grass, lis - ten - ing to our

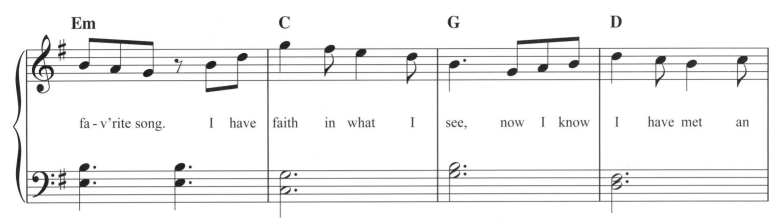

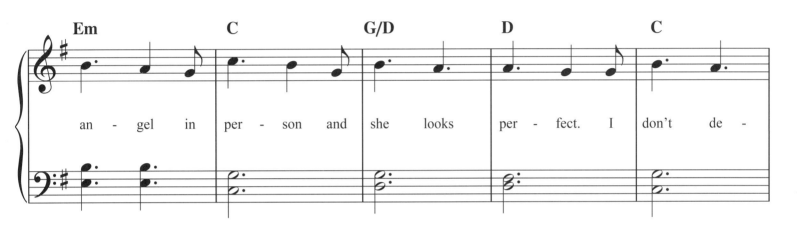

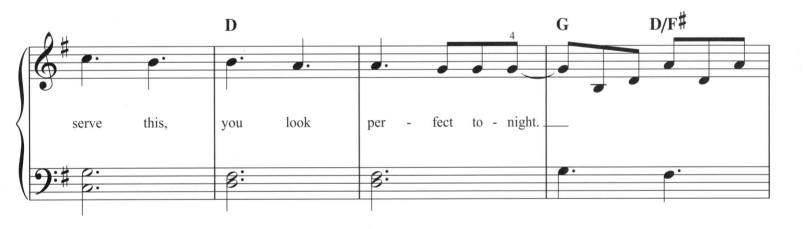

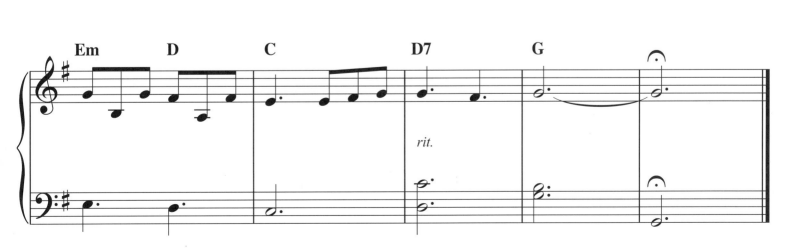

RADIOACTIVE

Words and Music by DANIEL REYNOLDS,
BENJAMIN McKEE, DANIEL SERMON,
ALEXANDER GRANT and JOSH MOSSER

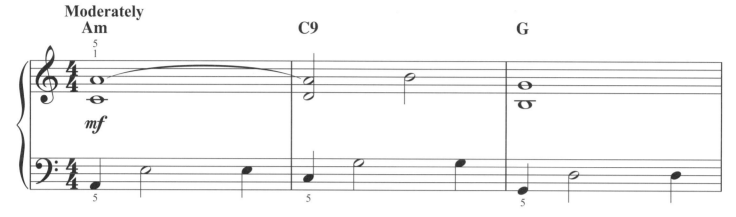

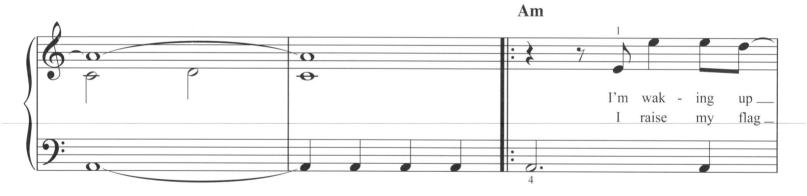

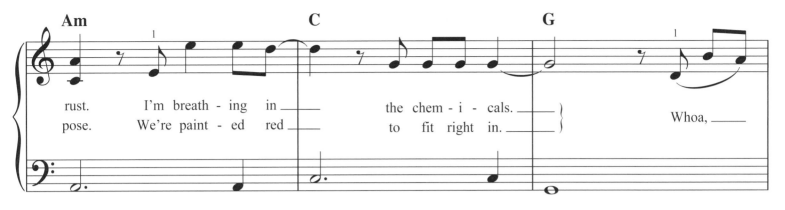

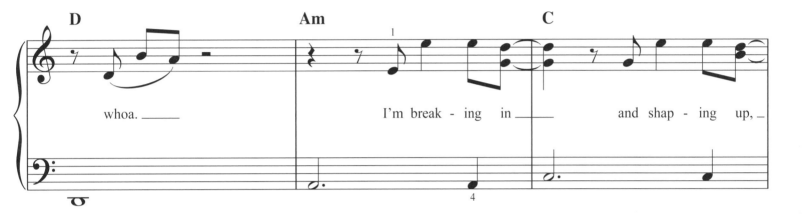

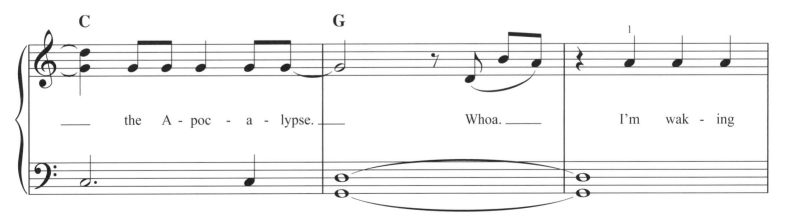

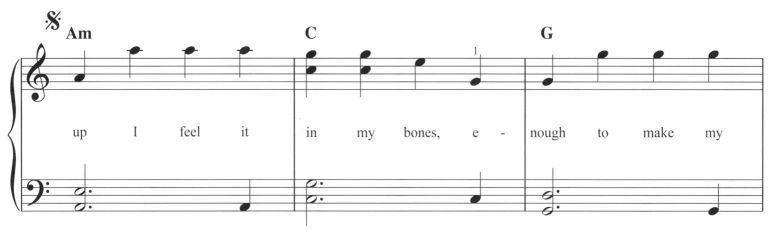

up I feel it in my bones, e - nough to make my

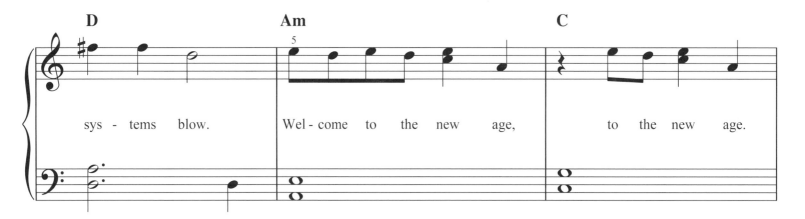

sys - tems blow. Wel - come to the new age, to the new age.

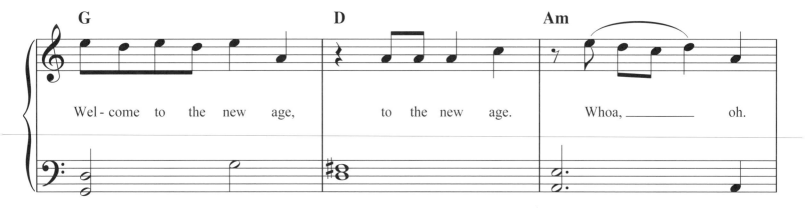

Wel - come to the new age, to the new age. Whoa, _____ oh.

Whoa _____ I'm ra - di - o - ac - tive, ra - di - o - ac - tive.

Whoa, _____ oh. Whoa, _____ I'm ra - di - o - ac - tive,

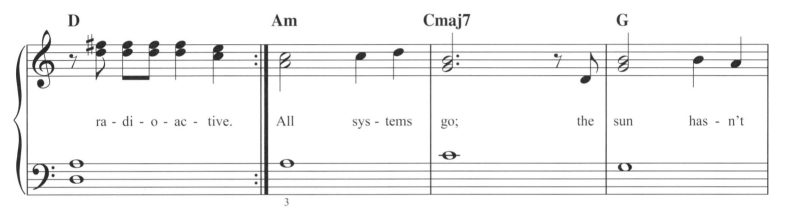

ra - di - o - ac - tive. All sys - tems go; the sun has - n't

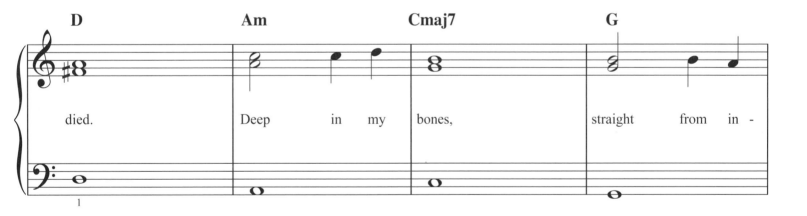

died. Deep in my bones, straight from in -

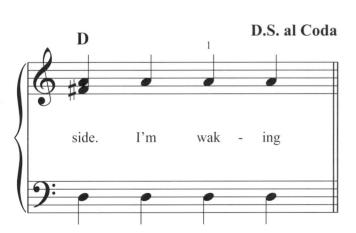

side. I'm wak - ing

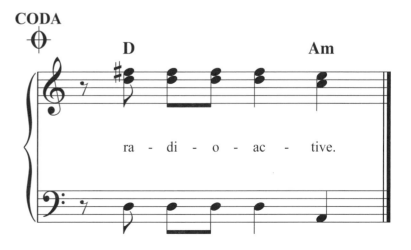

ra - di - o - ac - tive.

SHALLOW
from A STAR IS BORN

Words and Music by STEFANI GERMANOTTA,
MARK RONSON, ANDREW WYATT
and ANTHONY ROSSOMANDO

Moderately

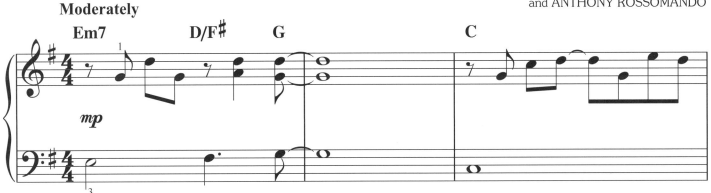

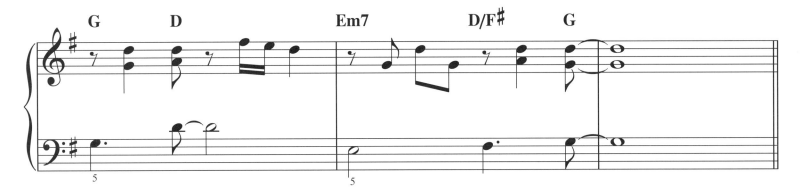

Tell me some-thing, girl: ___ are you hap-py in this
Tell me some-thing, boy: ___ aren't you tired, ___ tryin' to

mod-ern world, ___ or do you need more? ___
fill that void, ___ or do you need more? ___

Is there some-thing that you're search-ing for? ___
Ain't it hard keep-ing it so hard - core? ___
I'm fall - ing. ___

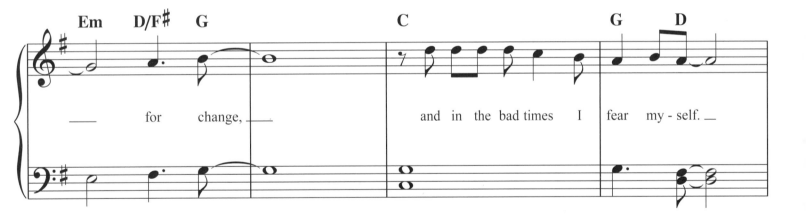

___ In all the good times I find my - self ___ long - ing ___

___ for change, ___ and in the bad times I fear my - self. ___

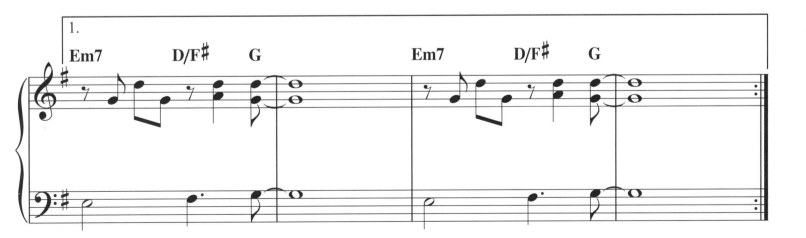

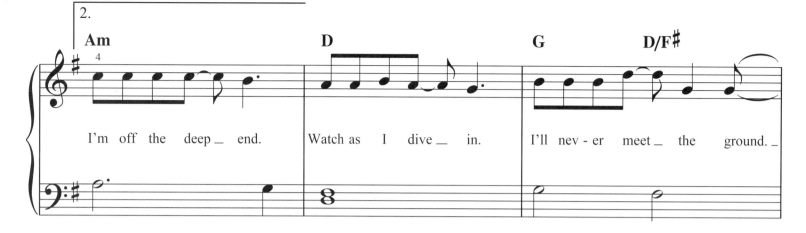

I'm off the deep __ end. Watch as I dive __ in. I'll nev - er meet __ the ground. __

__ Crash through the sur - face, where they can't hurt __ us. We're

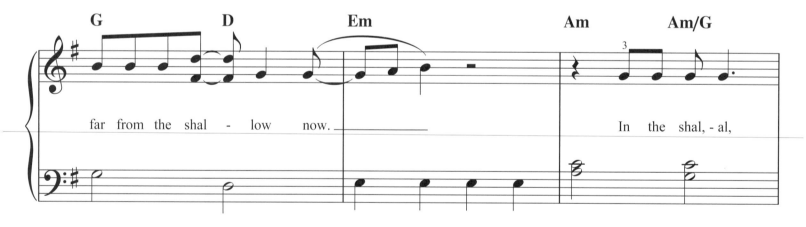

far from the shal - low now. __ In the shal, - al,

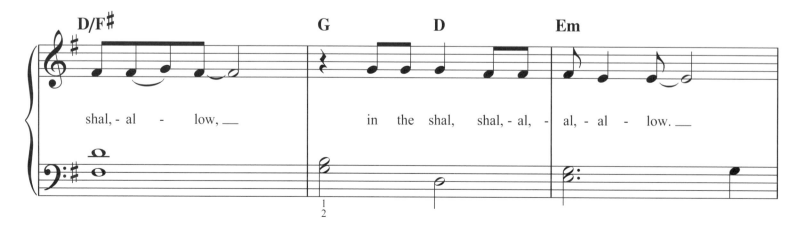

shal, - al - low, __ in the shal, shal, - al, - al - al - low. __

In the shal,-al,-shal,-al-low,— we're far from the shal-low now.

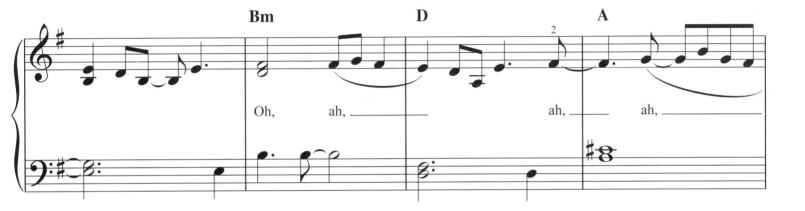

Oh, ah,____ ah,____ ah,

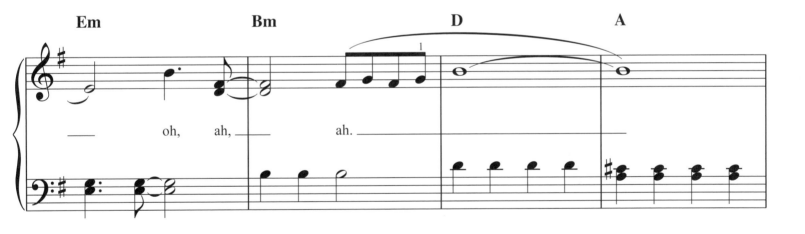

___ oh, ah,___ ah.___

I'm off the deep __ end. Watch as I dive __ in. I'll nev-er meet __ the ground. __

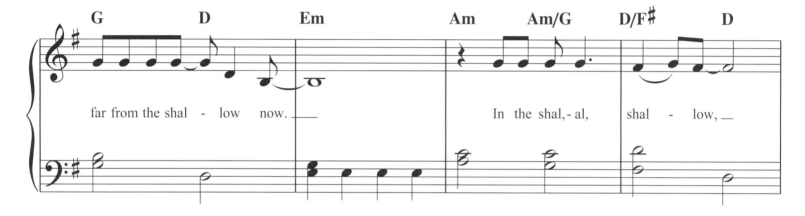

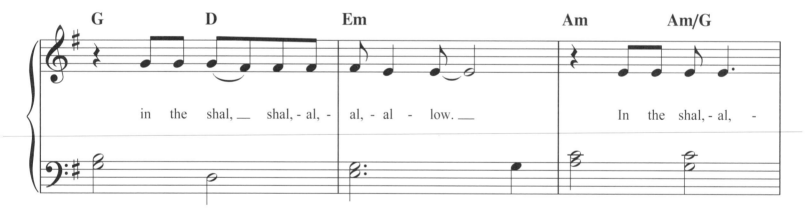

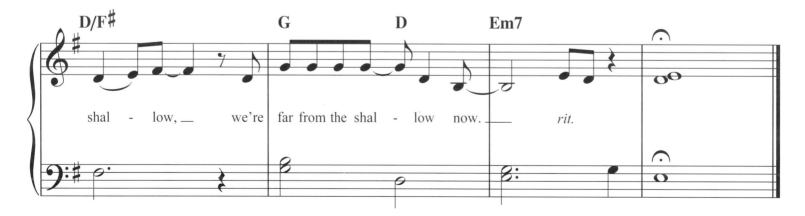

SOMEONE LIKE YOU

Words and Music by ADELE ADKINS
and DAN WILSON

Piano Ballad

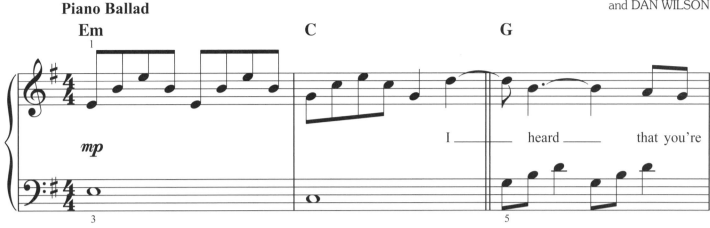

I ___ heard ___ that you're

set-tled down, that you   found a girl ___ and you're   mar-ried now. ___

___ I   heard ___   that your   dreams   came   true.   Guess she

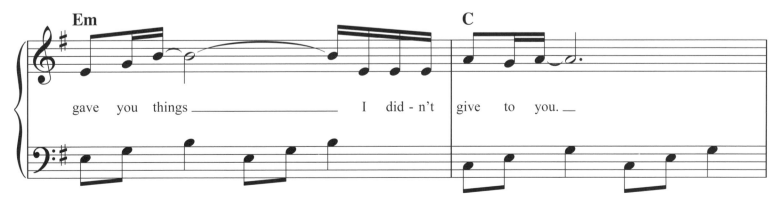

gave you things _____ I did-n't give to you. ___

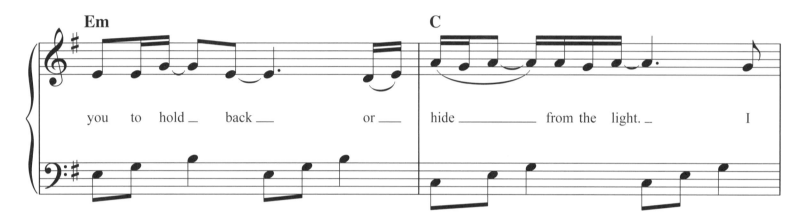

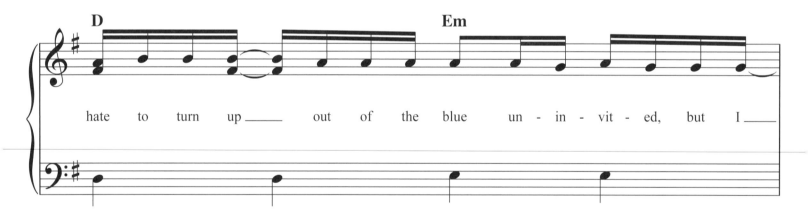

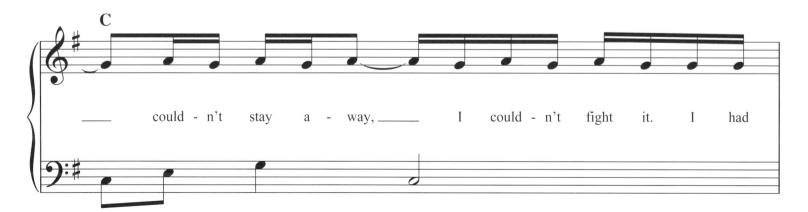

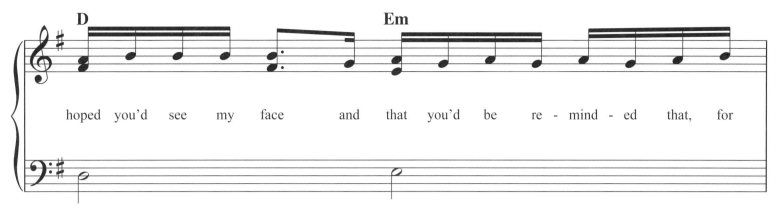

hoped you'd see my face and that you'd be re - mind - ed that, for

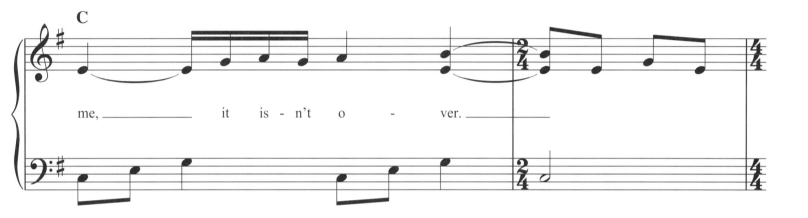

me, _____ it is - n't o - ver. _____

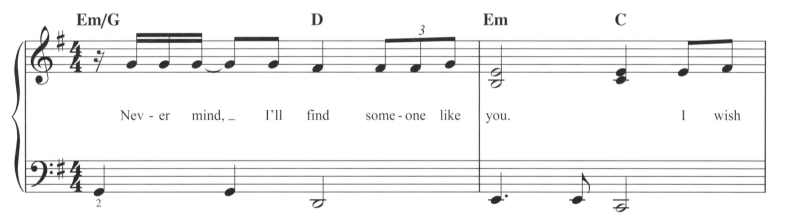

Nev - er mind, _ I'll find some - one like you. I wish

noth - ing but __ the best for you, too. Don't for - get me, I beg. I re -

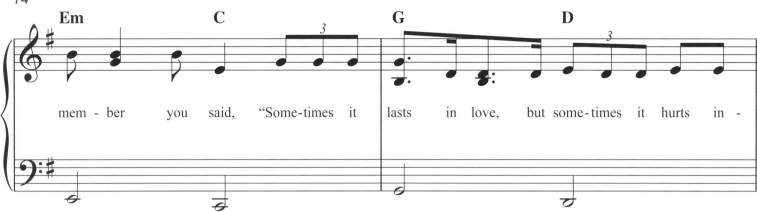

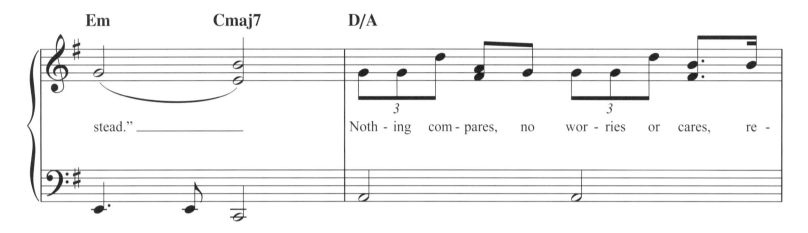

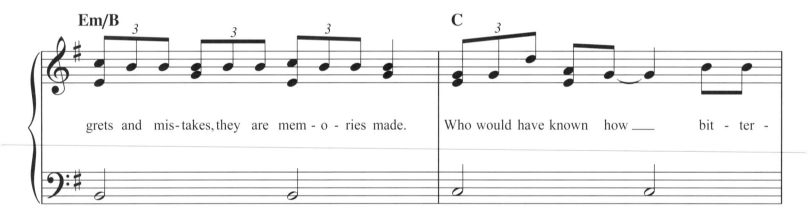

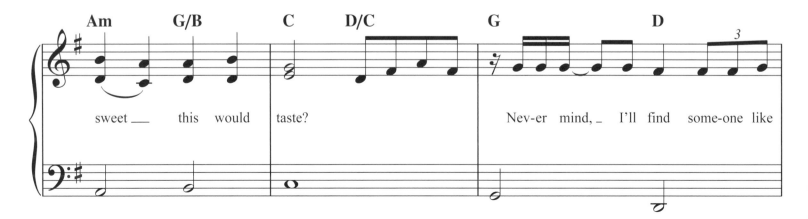

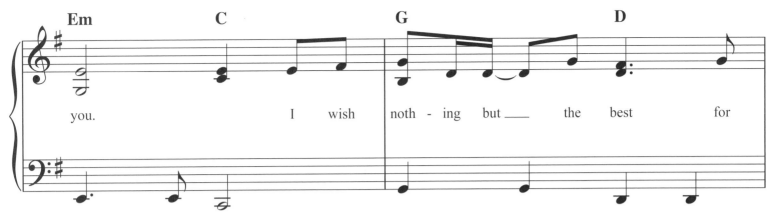

you. I wish noth - ing but ___ the best for

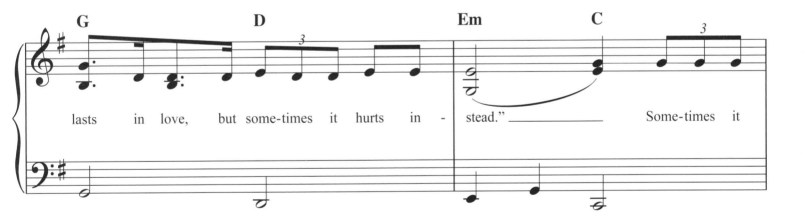

you, too. Don't for - get me, I beg. I ___ re - mem-ber you said, "Some-times it

lasts in love, but some-times it hurts in - stead." ___ Some-times it

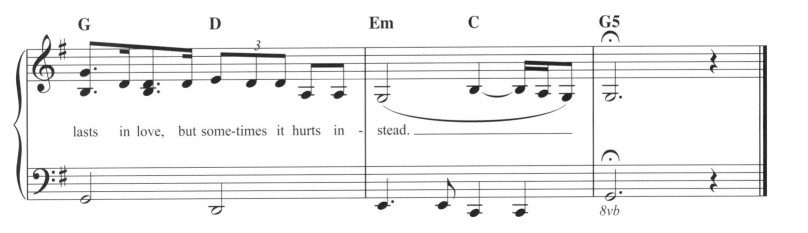

lasts in love, but some-times it hurts in - stead. ___

STARTING OVER

Words and Music by CHRIS STAPLETON
and MIKE HENDERSON

Well, the | road rolls out like a wel-come mat ___
might not be an ___ eas - y time. ___

to a | bet - ter place than the one we're at. | And
There's ___ riv-ers to cross and ___ hills to climb.

I ain't got no kind of plan, ___ | but I've | had all of this town I can stand.
Some days we might fall a - part, ___ | and | some nights ___ might feel cold and dark.

And   I got friends out on the coast. ____   We can
But   no-bod-y wins a-fraid of los-in', ____   and the

jump in the wa-ter and see ____ what floats.
hard roads   are ____ the ones ____ worth choos-in'.

D

We've been sav-in' for a rain-y day. ____   Let's
Some-day we'll look ____ back and smile, ____   and

beat the storm ____ and be on our way. }
know it was ____ worth ____ ev-'ry mile. }   And

it don't mat-ter to me; __ wher-ev-er we are is where I wan-na be. And,

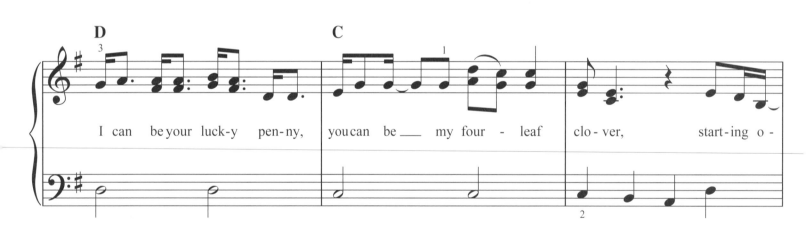

hon-ey, for once __ in our life, let's take our chanc-es and roll __ the dice. __

I can be your luck-y pen-ny, you can be __ my four-leaf clo-ver, start-ing o-

-ver. And this

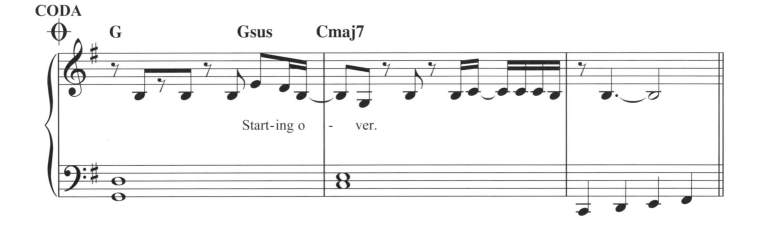

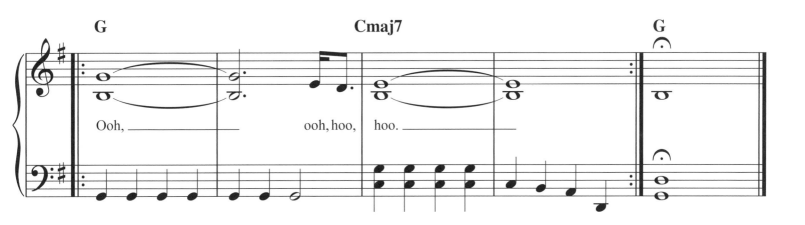

THEREFORE I AM

Words and Music by BILLIE EILISH O'CONNELL
and FINNEAS O'CONNELL

Moderate groove

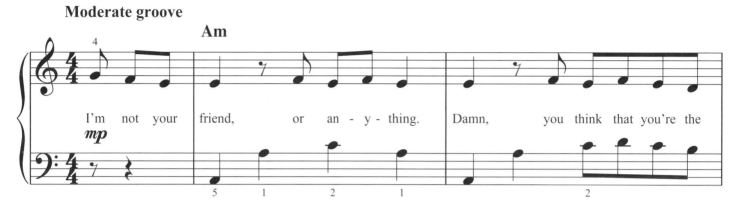

I'm not your friend, or an - y - thing. Damn, you think that you're the

man. __ I think, there - fore I am. __ I'm not your friend, or an - y - thing.

Damn, you think that you're the man. __ I think, there - fore I am. __

Stop. What the hell are you talk - ing a - bout? __ Ha! Get my pret - ty name out - ta your mouth. __

We are not the same, with or with-out. ___ Don't | talk 'bout me like how you might know how I feel. ___

Top of the world, __ but your world is-n't real. ___ Your world's an i - deal. ___ So, go have

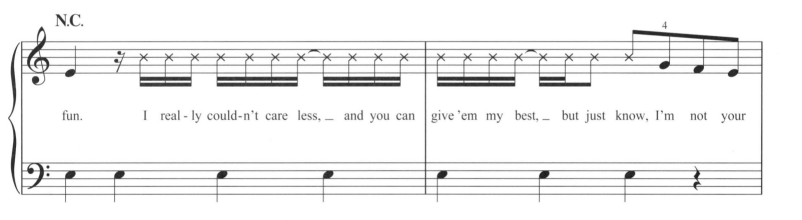

fun. I real - ly could-n't care less, __ and you can | give 'em my best, __ but just know, I'm not your

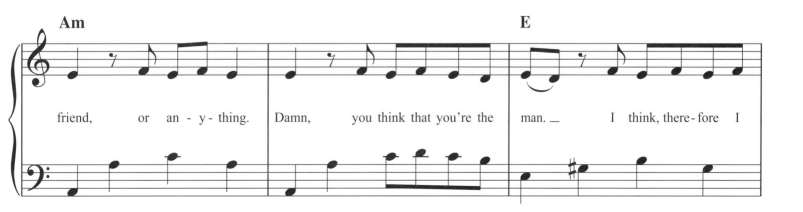

friend, or an - y - thing. Damn, you think that you're the | man. __ I think, there - fore I

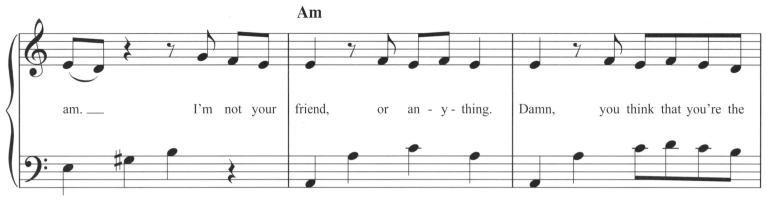

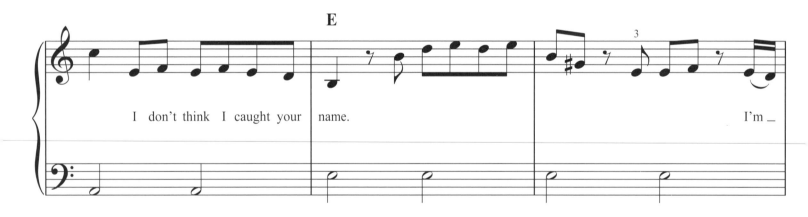

TREAT YOU BETTER

Words and Music by SHAWN MENDES,
SCOTT FRIEDMAN and TEDDY GEIGER

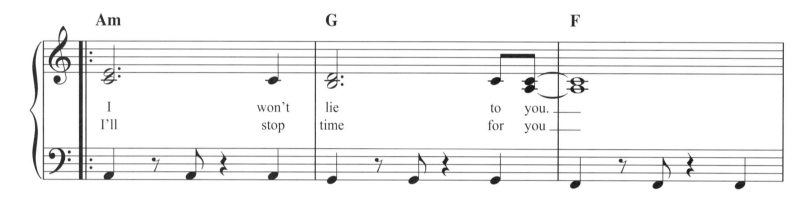

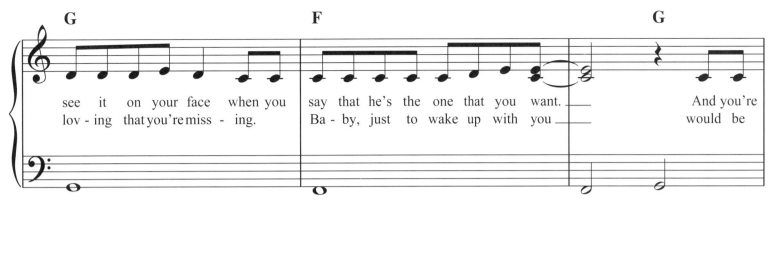

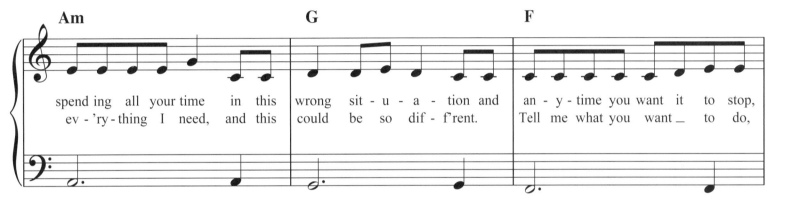

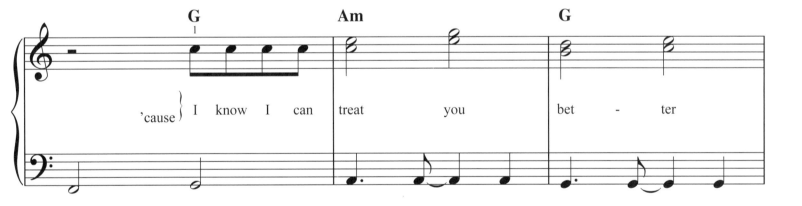

F ... **C** ... **G/B** ... **Am**

gen - tle - man.   Tell me why are we   wast - ing time __ on all your

G ... **F** ... **C** ... **G/B**

wast - ed   cryin' __ when you should   be with   me __ in - stead?   I know I can

Am ... **G** ... **F**

treat   you   bet - ter,   bet - ter than __ he can.

Am ... **G** ... **F** ... **C**

Bet - ter than __ he can.

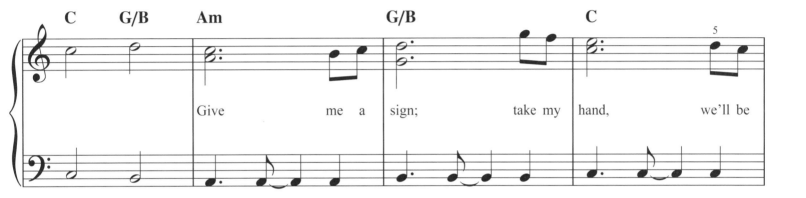

Give me a sign; take my hand, we'll be

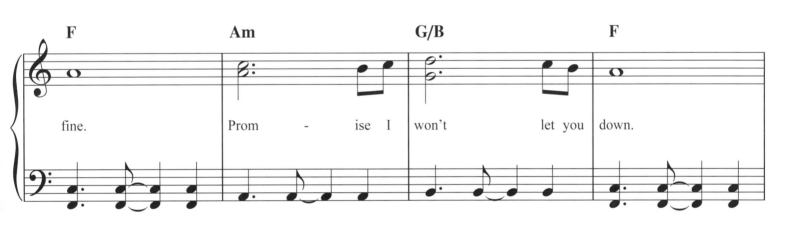

fine. Prom - ise I won't let you down.

Just know that you don't have to do this a -

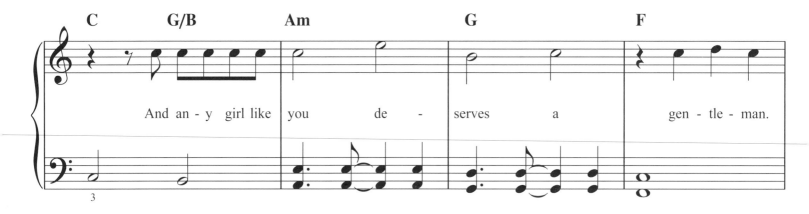

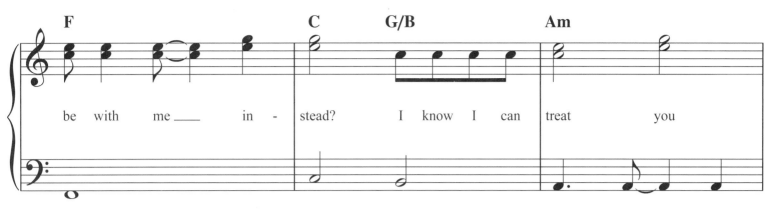

be with me — in - stead? I know I can treat you

bet - ter, better than — he can.

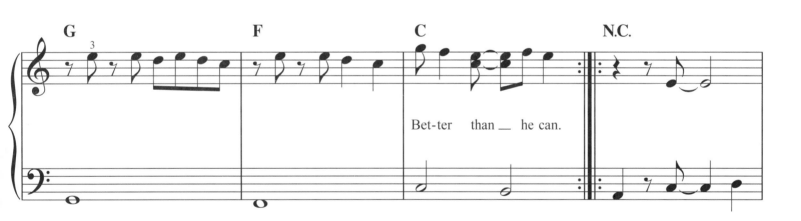

Bet-ter than — he can.

WE ARE WARRIORS
(Warrior)

Words and Music by AVRIL LAVIGNE,
CHAD KROEGER and TRAVIS CLARK

Moderately slow

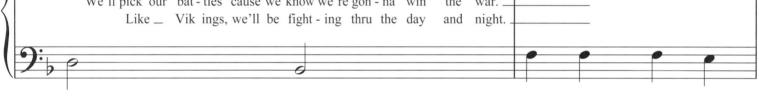

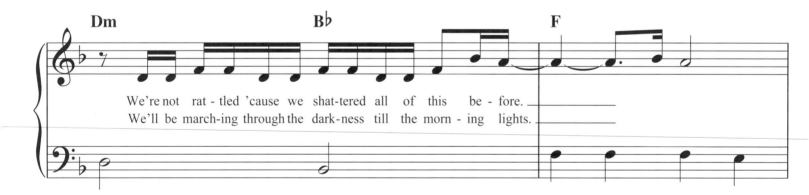

We'll pick our bat - tles 'cause we know we're gon - na win the war.
Like _ Vik ings, we'll be fight - ing thru the day and night.

We're not rat - tled 'cause we shat - tered all of this be - fore.
We'll be march-ing through the dark-ness till the morn - ing lights.

Stead - i - er than steel 'cause we're read - y with our shield and sword.
E - ven when it's hard - er, like the ar - mor, you will see us shine.

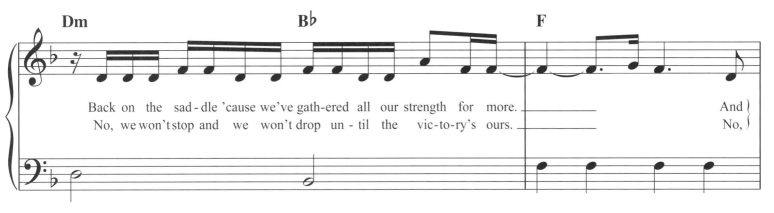

Back on the sad - dle 'cause we've gath-ered all our strength for more. _____ And
No, we won't stop and we won't drop un - til the vic-to-ry's ours. _____ No,

we won't bow, we won't break. No, we're not a - fraid to do what-ev - er it takes. We'll

nev - er bow, we'll nev - er break. _____ 'Cause we are war-ri-ors, _ we'll fight _ for our lives _ like

sol - diers, _ all _____ thru the night. _ And we won't give up, _ we _____ will sur - vive. _ We are

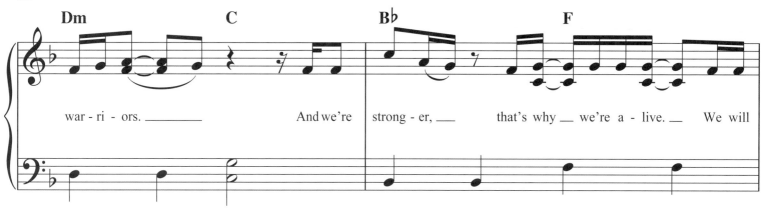

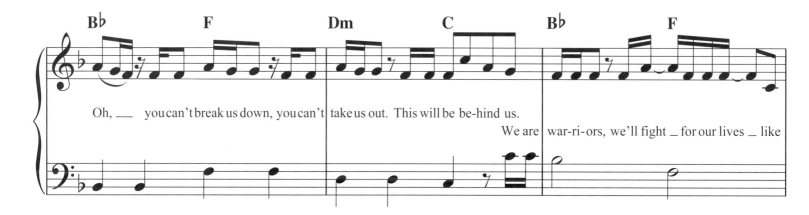

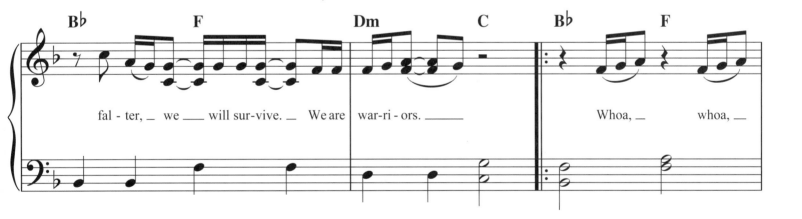

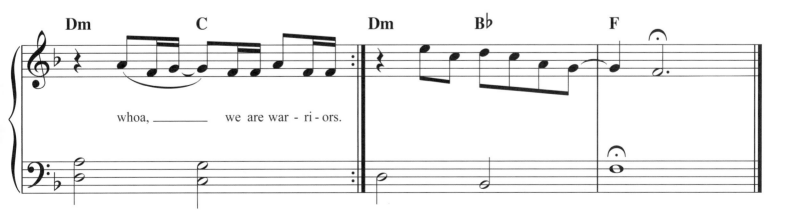

WILLOW

Words and Music by TAYLOR SWIFT
and AARON DESSNER

Moderately, in 2

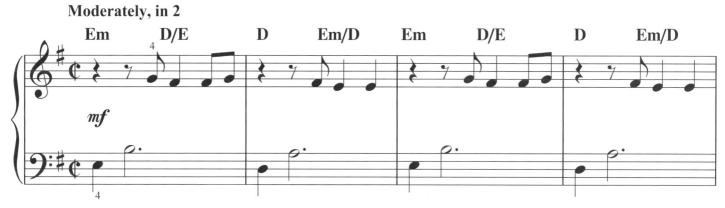

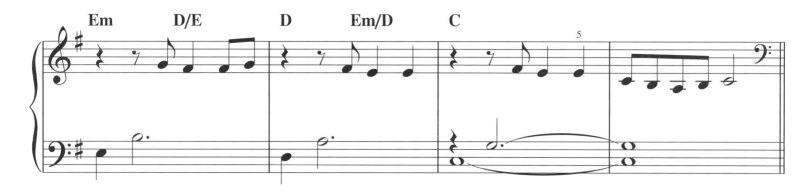

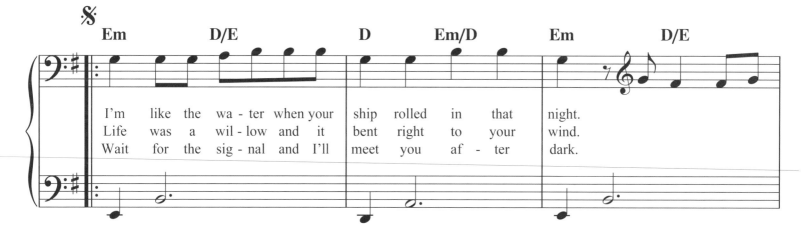

I'm like the wa-ter when your ship rolled in that night.
Life was a wil-low and it bent right to your wind.
Wait for the sig-nal and I'll meet you af-ter dark.

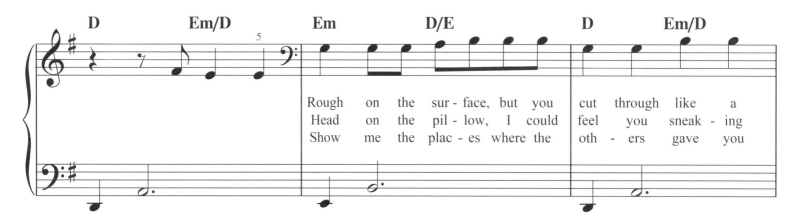

Rough on the sur-face, but you cut through like a
Head on the pil-low, I could feel you sneak-ing
Show me the plac-es where the oth-ers gave you

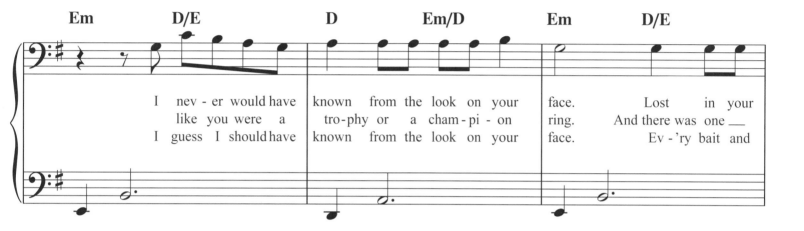

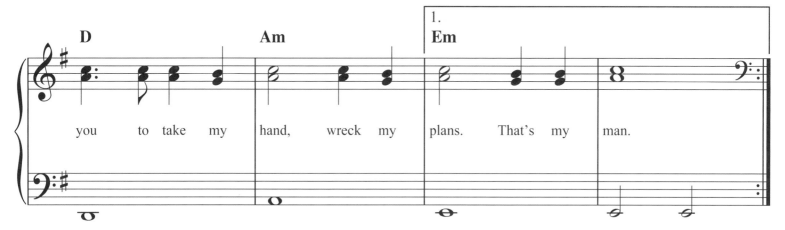

you to take my hand, wreck my plans. That's my man.

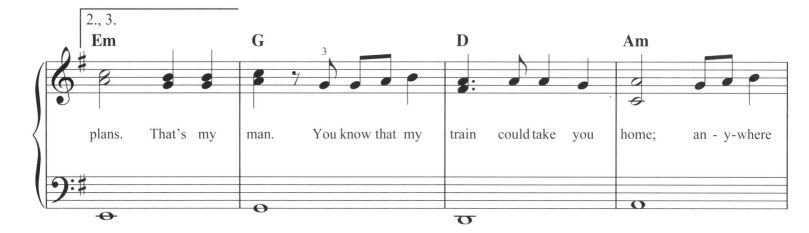

plans. That's my man. You know that my train could take you home; an-y-where

else is hol - low. I'm beg-ging for you to take my hand, wreck my

plans. That's my man.

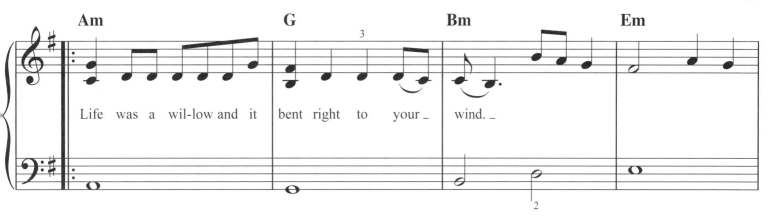

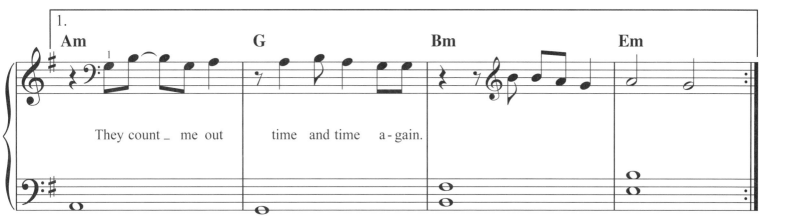

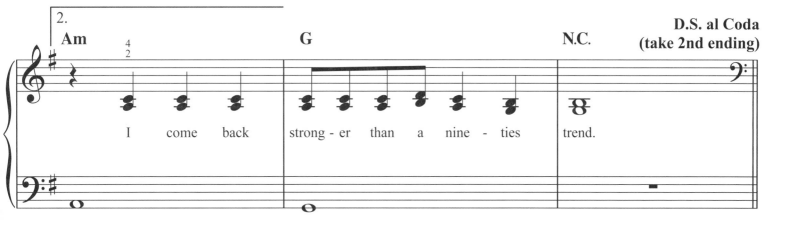

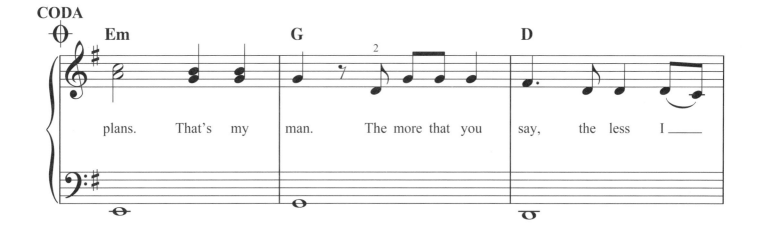

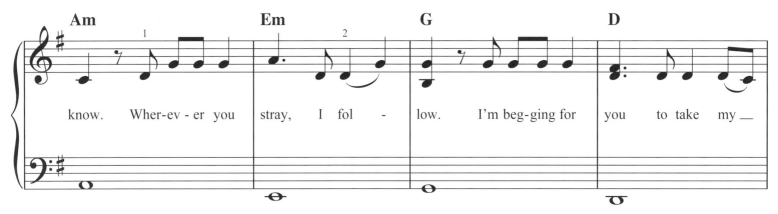

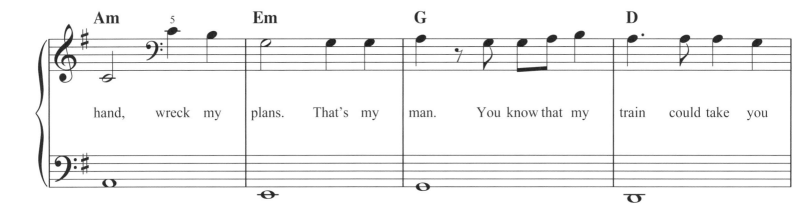

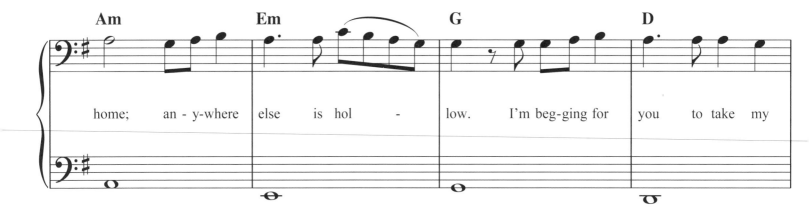

man.   Yeah, that's my   man.   Yeah, that's   my

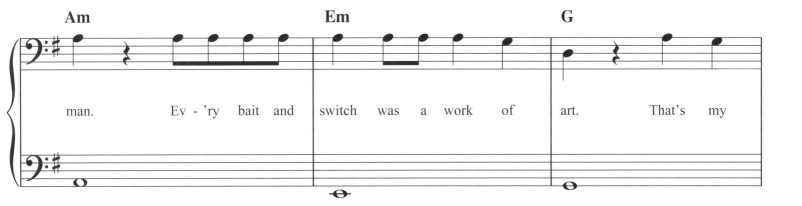

man.   Ev-'ry bait and   switch was   a   work   of   art.   That's   my

man.   Hey, _ that's my   man.   I'm beg-ging for

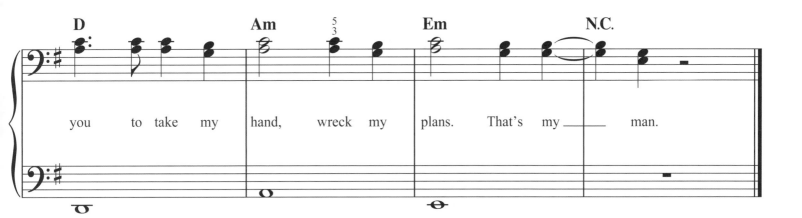

you   to take my   hand,   wreck my   plans.   That's my ___ ___ man.

WONDER

Words and Music by SHAWN MENDES,
THOMAS HULL, SCOTT HARRIS
and NATE MERCEREAU

Pop Rock

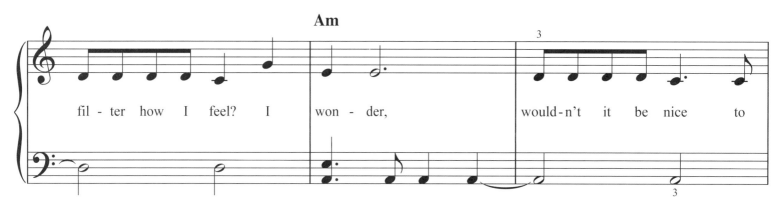

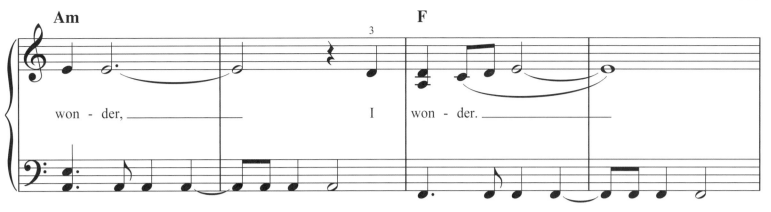

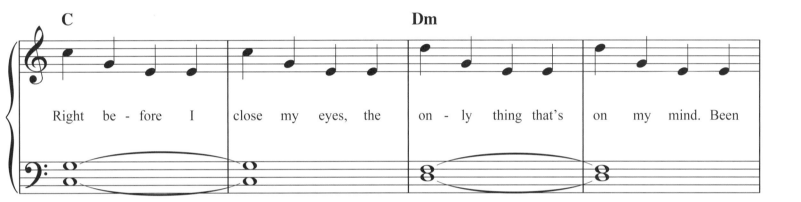

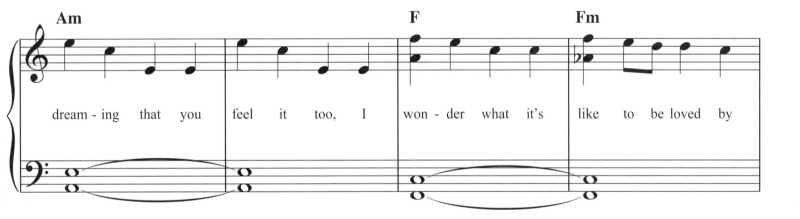

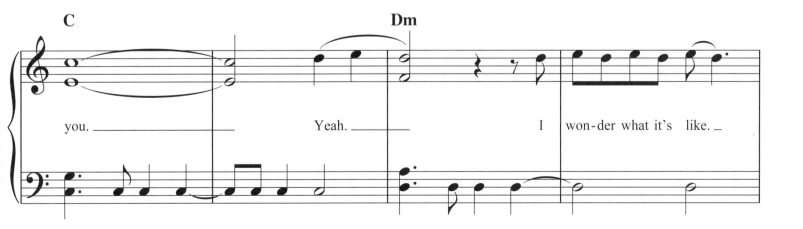

Yeah. _____ I won-der what it's like _ to be loved by you, yeah.

I won-der what it's like to be loved by... Right be-fore I

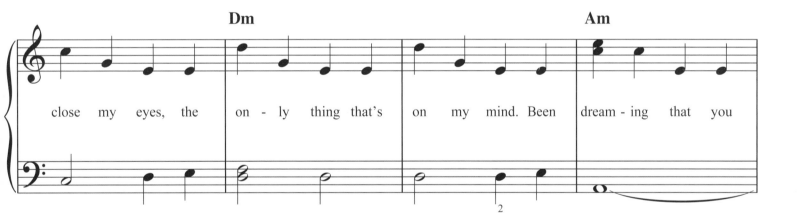

close my eyes, the on - ly thing that's on my mind. Been dream - ing that you

feel it too, I won - der what it's like to be loved by you.

YOU SAY

Words and Music by LAUREN DAIGLE,
JASON INGRAM and PAUL MABURY

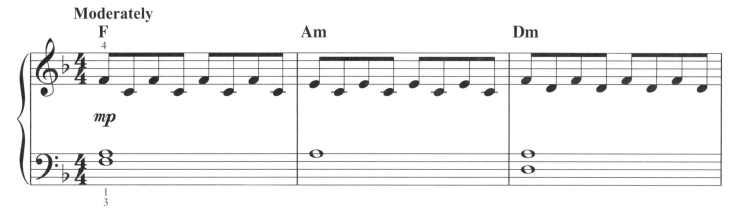

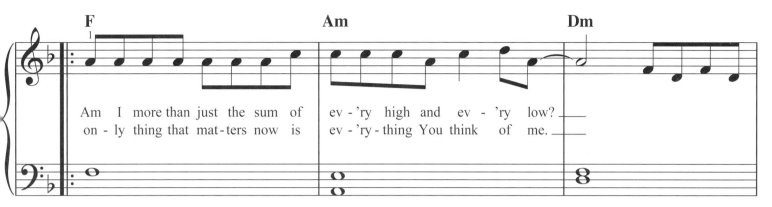

held   when I am fall-ing   short.   And when I don't be - long,   oh, You say I am

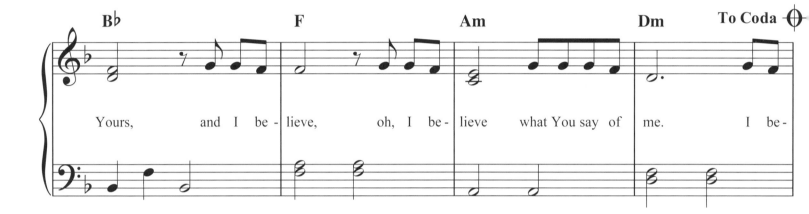

Yours,   and I be - lieve,   oh, I be - lieve   what You say of   me.   I be-

lieve.   The   lieve.   Tak-ing all I have, and now I'm

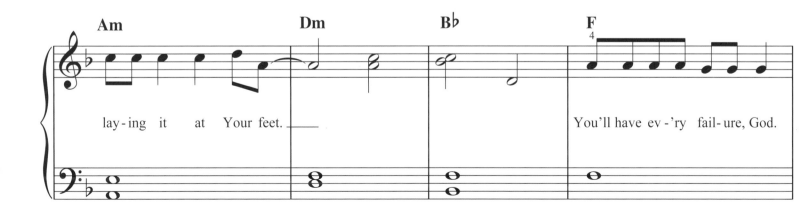

lay - ing it   at Your feet.____   You'll have ev -'ry fail-ure, God.

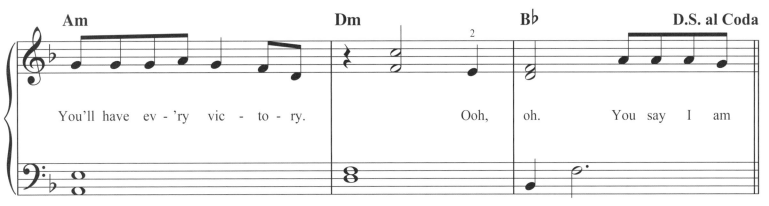

SOMEONE YOU LOVED

Words and Music by LEWIS CAPALDI,
BENJAMIN KOHN, PETER KELLEHER,
THOMAS BARNES and SAMUEL ROMAN

I'm go-ing un-der, and this time I fear there's no one to save
I'm go-ing un-der, and this time I fear there's no one to turn

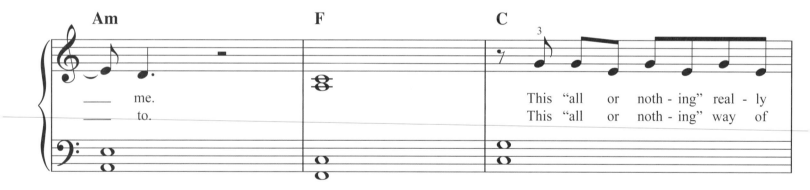

me.
to.

This "all or noth-ing" real-ly
This "all or noth-ing" way of

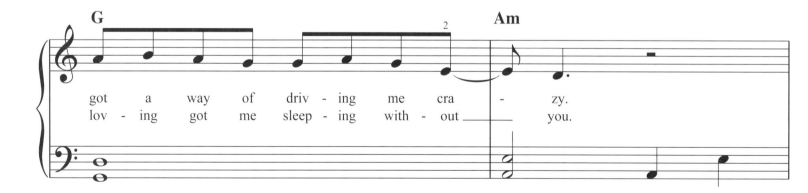

got a way of driv-ing me cra - zy.
lov-ing got me sleep-ing with-out you.

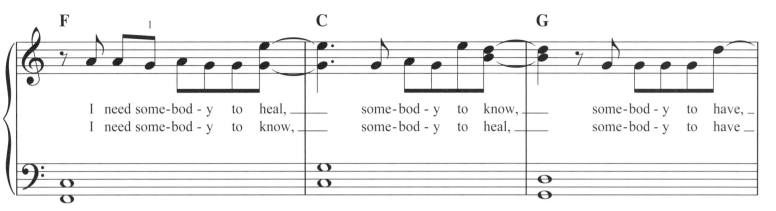

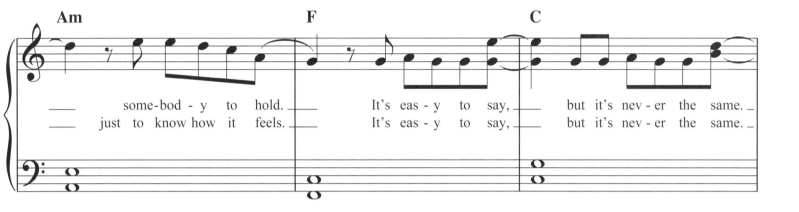

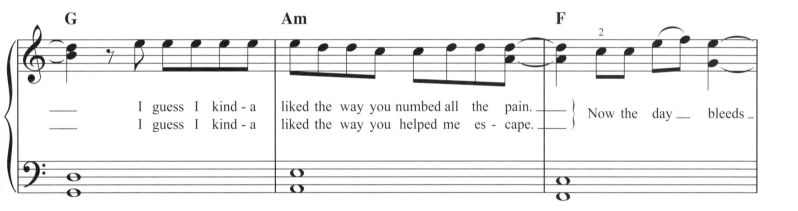

I let my guard down, and then you pulled the rug. I was get-ting kind-a

used to be-ing some-one you loved. And

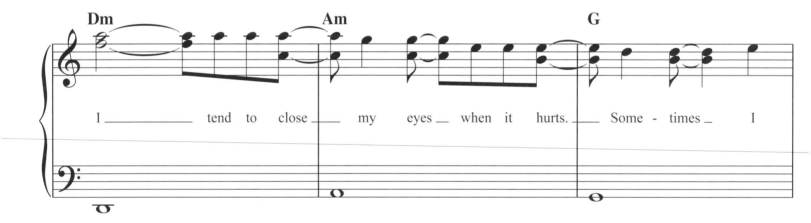

I tend to close my eyes when it hurts. Some-times I

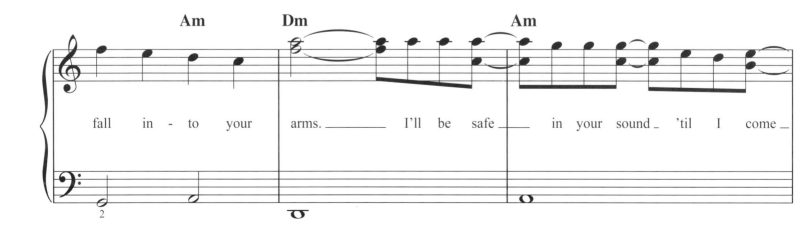

fall in-to your arms. I'll be safe in your sound 'til I come